ROMAN
ENGLAND

COLCHESTER
J.H.P.

A face-urn found at Colchester, dating from the first or second century.

ROMAN ENGLAND

JOHN BURKE

ARTUS BOOKS
LONDON

ISBN 1 85605 166 8
Printed in Italy

CONTENTS

Birth of the sun-god Mithras, from the third-century temple near Carrawburgh fort on Hadrian's Wall.

THE COMING OF THE ROMANS

WHEN Julius Caesar decided in 55 BC to launch an attack on the southern coast of the land which the Romans called Britannia, he had two main reasons. One was the need to punish Belgic settlers in these islands for the support they were giving to their rebellious cousins in mainland Gaul, the Celtic territories west of the Alps between the Rhine and the Mediterranean which today largely make up France and the Low Countries. The other motive was greed: the inhabitants carried on a profitable export trade in tin, lead and corn, and Caesar fancied bringing all this under Roman control.

He sent emissaries to win over local rulers where possible, but found it difficult to get a clear picture of the situation because of differences between the earlier British peoples and the later Belgic settlers. Some tribal chieftains were eager to deal peaceably with Rome and win favours. Others defiantly offered shelter to refugees from alien domination. In spite of uncertainties, Caesar gambled on there being enough factions to collaborate or at least keep out of his way if he decided to invade. With two legions of about 5000 men each he set off in the autumn of 55 and landed somewhere between Deal and Walmer in Kent.

The landing was not a great success. Native forces were driven back but could not be decisively beaten because a sudden storm held the Roman cavalry transports off, and those ships which had already been hauled ashore were heavily battered. In spite of this, Caesar engaged the natives once again, received offers of submission from some chieftains, and took hostages back to Gaul.

Next summer he tried again with five instead of two legions, plus some 2000 cavalry. This time they came ashore between Deal and Sandwich. Caesar left his ships and made a forced march upon Britons assembled at a crossing of the river Stour. The tribesmen tried to hold out in the hill-fort whose ramparts still stand at Bigbury, two miles (3.2 km) west of Canterbury, but were overrun. The victors

set about building a base camp before pressing on with the campaign, only to be interrupted by news that the previous year's disaster had been repeated: a storm had driven their ships on to the beach and completely smashed about 40 of them.

While Caesar was coping with repairs, the scattered defenders rallied under the leadership of Cassivellaunus, chieftain of the Catuvellauni tribe which held sway over a large area north of the river Thames. By the time Caesar was ready to resume hostilities a great force of war chariots had been built up that created havoc among the Roman cavalry until new tactics were adopted to cope with

Julius Caesar, who subdued large parts of Europe but made only limited inroads on south-eastern Britain.

7

such onslaughts. Unfortunately for these daring warriors, their leader had some time before killed the king of the neighbouring Trinovantes and driven his son into exile in Gaul. The stricken tribe and a number of smaller groups now offered submission to Caesar if he would restore the young prince and subdue their mutual enemy.

With the help of local intelligence Caesar closed in on the hidden Catuvellaunian *oppidum*, or fortress, about half a mile (0.8 km) south-west of Wheathampstead in Hertfordshire. Fighting was fierce but for a while inconclusive. Cassivellaunus tried to create a diversion by appealing to Kentish leaders to destroy the remainder of the beached Roman galleys. When this last throw failed he was forced to surrender.

News of unrest on the mainland called for Caesar's speedy return. He arranged treaties with several British chieftains, took hostages, and exacted a promise of regular payments of tribute in return for his guarantee of protection against any future native aggressor. There was a clear warning that in the event of any lapse the legions would soon be back; and in any case it was planned to occupy the entire country in due course and make it a Roman province.

Such plans took a long time to mature. Trade continued briskly enough, and some tribal aristocrats grew wealthy and acquired Romanized tastes after bartering their produce for glass, pottery,

A gold aureus *struck in honour of Claudius, featuring a triumphal arch on the reverse with the words* De Britann *surmounted by a Celtic horse goddess, Epona.*

jewellery and other luxuries. In 24 BC the historian and geographer Strabo wrote of corn, cattle, gold, silver and iron being shipped from Britain, 'also hides, slaves, and clever hunting dogs'. The mineral and agricultural resources were still there for the taking; but conflicts in occupied territories and in Rome itself meant the postponement of any follow-up to that brief reconnaissance of southern Britain. Although payments of tribute were neglected and local wars broke out in spite of Julius Caesar's guarantees, it was almost a century before his successors began again to consider full-scale annexation.

Early in the first century AD a powerful ruler had begun his own bit of empire-building. Cunobelinus (Shakespeare's 'Cymbeline') harassed rival chieftains and took over their peoples, land, and trade. After his death his territories in eastern and south-eastern Britain and what are now Bedfordshire, Oxfordshire and a large part of the Home Counties were shared out between his sons Togodumnus and Caratacus, who did not slacken in the persecution of their weaker neighbours. Some victims fled to Rome and appealed for old treaties to be honoured. The princelings' own exiled brother, Adminius, urged an invasion and offered to work with the Roman forces.

In AD 42 Messalina, wife of the Emperor Claudius, presented him with a son who was given the name Britannicus. The recently proclaimed

A stater, *a gold coin with the abbreviated names of Camulodunum (Colchester) and Cunobelinus. It shows tribal symbols of an ear of corn and a horse.*

This glass flagon and blue-and-white marbled bowl were found in a first-century grave at Radnage, Buckinghamshire.

The main tribal territories at the time of Claudius's invasion.

Roman legionaries march across a bridge improvised from boats, led by their standard-bearers.

emperor, still unsure of his position and needing a dramatic gesture to consolidate his shaky hold on power, decided the time was ripe for military adventure. Four legions and a large force of auxiliaries were assembled near Boulogne in the late spring of AD 43 and, after what seems to have been a token mutiny on the grounds that they were being asked to serve 'beyond the inhabited world', were persuaded to set sail.

The solid core of the Roman army consisted of long-serving professional infantry, recruited on a voluntary basis from full Roman citizens. A man would serve for 25 years and retire with a substantial gratuity, part of it often in the form of a house and a smallholding. Each legion numbered 4800 men, divided into 10 cohorts of 480, with a further subdivision into maniples of 160. Half of a maniple was known as a century, though it was officially 80 and not 100 men. As with modern regiments, a legion was not invariably up to full strength, or on occasion had been reinforced with extra manpower,

so that numbers could in reality vary between 4000 and 5000.

To supplement the regulars there were auxiliary units recruited or conscripted from the provinces. Such levies were not full citizens but stood a good chance of becoming so after 25 years' service. They provided infantrymen known as *cohortes*, who were usually thrown into an attack before the highly trained crack troops advanced to finish the job, and cavalry units known as *alae*, or wings, because of their use on the wings of the main force. Formations serving abroad had as commander-in-chief a proconsul, acting on behalf of the two regal magistrates or consuls who 'consulted' (or in effect manipulated) the Roman senate. The proconsul would as a rule delegate powers to a legate, the equivalent of a general, whose staff consisted of military tribunes and, immediately below them, the centurions who each commanded a century.

The general in charge of Claudius's invasion force was Aulus Plautius, who had served with

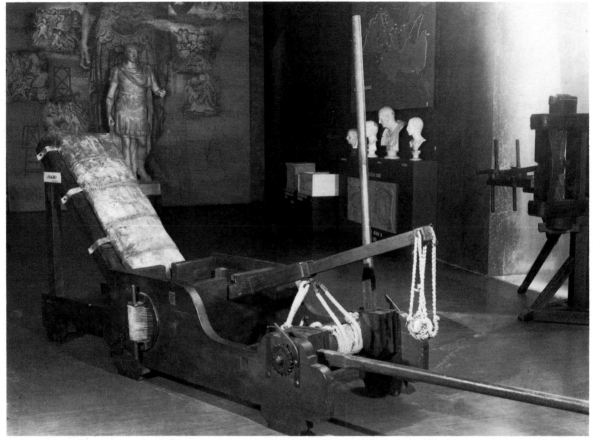

An onager, a war catapult powered by the torsion of twisted ropes to hurl heavy stones. It was so named because it kicked like an onager or wild ass.

distinction as governor of Pannonia in the Danube basin. From remarks in a sketchy surviving record of the time it has been suggested that he split his fleet into three, one part of which made a landing in the welcoming territory of an allied king near Chichester Harbour in Sussex. This has never been backed up by archaeological evidence, and even if in fact a couple of subsidiary landings did take place there is little doubt that the invasion effectively began at Rutupiae (Richborough) in Kent. Reconnaissance had shown this to offer a more reliable anchorage than the open beaches where Julius Caesar had twice almost come to grief, and it was destined to become the army's main supply port.

Little resistance was met in the immediate vicinity. Plautius had time to build a fort near the old stronghold at Bigbury before setting off to cross the Medway, probably near Rochester. Here a hastily assembled army was waiting ready to do battle under Togodumnus. It was soon driven back to the Thames, where Togodumnus died in another skirmish.

The commander felt secure enough to wait for Claudius himself to travel to Britain and have the satisfaction of marching with his troops upon the Catuvellaunian capital of Camulodunum (Colchester) and witnessing its downfall. The remaining warlord Caratacus, however, managed to escape, and for some years was to harry the occupying power from strongholds in the Welsh mountains. Plautius made no immediate attempt to pursue him but divided his forces for a three-pronged advance on Lindum (Lincoln) to the north, into the Midlands, and westwards to the hill-forts of Hod Hill, Maiden Castle, and beyond.

Claudius decreed that Colchester should be the capital of the new province, nominally under his direct personal control but in fact to be administered by a legate with the help of financial and legal officers. A separate procurator was made directly responsible to the emperor for tax collection.

A bronze diploma from Malpas, Cheshire, granting a time-expired Spanish auxiliary in AD 103 full citizenship and the right to marry.

Within four years the invaders had established themselves across southern England and as far north and west as a diagonal line through Bath, Leicester and Lincoln. This frontier was marked by a military road now known as the Foss Way because of the deep adjacent *fossae* or ditches from which its basic material was dug. Much of the original route is followed today by the A429, though some deviating stretches have been reduced to nothing more than overgrown tracks. Other roads were linked to this highway, and at High Cross in Leicestershire a stone pillar erected in 1712, now in a private garden, marks the spot where Watling Street crosses it on the way from Canterbury and London to Wroxeter in Shropshire. Once this was claimed to be the precise centre of England.

An efficient road system was top priority in every

The tombstone of a standard-bearer from York.

Within the defences of the original bridgehead fort at Richborough is the

base of a great column erected to celebrate the conquest of southern Britain.

Ditches and wall at Richborough, added when the coast was threatened by Saxon invaders and rival would-be emperors.

Roman conquest. Swift movement of the legions was essential during a campaign, and once a country had been invested there was still the need to police the new territories and keep forts and population centres supplied with food and equipment. In Britannia there were eventually well over 6000 miles of highway and side roads.

Basic construction varied little. An *agger*, or embankment, was built with materials excavated from beside the route, leaving ditches which were useful for drainage. Occasionally stone might be brought from some distance to provide a solid layer on which gravel, broken flints or smaller stones would be laid. In iron-working areas the hard slag left over from smelting provided ideal metalling. Alignment of the route was carried out with remarkable accuracy, considering the lack of modern surveying instruments. Although many trackways were in existence when they arrived, the Roman military engineers rarely adapted these to their own uses. They preferred to start afresh and plot straight, disciplined lengths from successive high points. If it was necessary to get round an obstacle this was done not by following the twists of natural contours but by constructing shorter straight lengths. Major changes of direction were usually achieved on high ground from which sighting of the next stretch could most efficiently be carried out.

Supervision of the newly subjugated vassals was effected from forts and subsidiary camps. Some were built before the roads reached them, others were duly placed at strategic points along those roads. The standard Roman fort was a rectangle which might start with a ditch from which earth was dug for a rampart; this was then topped with a timber palisade, and later strengthened with stone if available. Inside would be barrack blocks, a headquarters building, and workshops for the craftsmen who always travelled with the army. Smaller staging camps and posting stations could manage with just the fundamental earthworks and palisade. Signal stations kept one camp in touch with the other by means of fiery beacons at night and smoke signalling by day.

Adjoining the more firmly established forts and camps there inevitably grew up shanty towns from which civilian traders supplied the troops with food, goods, and probably feminine company. Like railway junctions in the nineteenth century they often provided the focus for a growing community which remained capable of supporting itself after the original stimulus had died away.

Roman governors were charged with integrating local communities and customs as smoothly as possible into their own prescribed pattern of existence. Within overall imperial control it was more fruitful to coax natives into willing cooperation on everyday matters than to allocate armed battalions to keep them in permanent bondage. At the start the conquerors sought to create alliances with tribal leaders and win them over as 'client kings' who would be granted their own capitals and a large measure of self-government. A settlement of traders and camp followers was accorded humbler status as a *vicus*, the lowest class of town to which powers of government were granted, with a few administrative concessions. A rural district of peasant farmers with no particular centre such as a tribal capital or market town was classified as a *pagus*.

The province remained primarily agricultural. There were iron workings in the Weald of Kent and Sussex, and in the Forest of Dean; tin was mined in Cornwall, lead in the Midlands and the north; a state weaving mill was established at Venta Belgarum (Winchester); and local potteries learned new skills from European models. But most of the population continued to work in the fields, some in small communities as before, and some in more extensive villas that offered greater possibilities of assimilation into the Roman régime. As well as providing supply lines for the military, the new roads facilitated the transport of produce by native traders, importers, and exporters – though naturally at suitable points there were tax collecting offices, often at road junctions serving the villas of farmers who had been here before the Romans came and who now went on much in their old style, though with the additional burden of paying imperial tribute and feeding the legions.

Early in 1983, while this book was in preparation, archaeologists unearthed what they thought must be the first Roman tax collection depot authenticated in Britain. It was at Claydon Pike in the Thames valley and appears to have been set up around 70 A D, remaining in service right until the end of the Roman occupation.

The Latin word *villa* means simply a farm, but has come to be applied to the residential heart of the estate. It was in no sense a holiday home or weekend retreat for town-dwellers but the hub of a working community. When a local dignitary had to serve for stipulated periods on official duties in a town he might appoint a *vilicus*, or bailiff, to run the property in his absence. This would add to his financial responsibilities, for he would still be required to produce his quota of crops for the army, pay taxes on any remaining profits, and at the same time maintain a town residence.

A Roman legionary with segmented iron or bronze armour, a helmet with cheek-guards, and carrying a pilum *or javelin.*

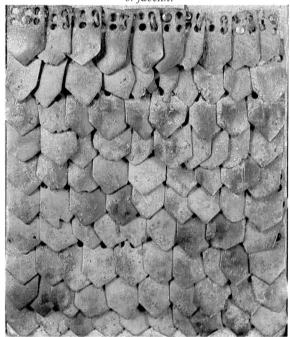

A fragment of scale armour found in Northumberland.

VILLAS

Some villas were merely adaptations of tribal huts that were added to either as the family grew in numbers or prosperity, or from a desire to emulate the Roman way of life. Romano-British magnates became ashamed of their primitive round wooden farmhouses and started to construct rectangular cottages with two or three small rooms connected by inner doorways that were still wooden at first but made increasing use of stone and mortar. Within half a century of the occupation it was common to find internal corridors with rooms to either side, or an outer veranda serving the same purpose. Rooms and passages could be extended in various directions and a spacious central dining-room became a feature of more ambitious homes. Wings were added to embrace a yard or ornamental garden, and examples have been unearthed of villas with two enclosed courtyards, one functional and the other for private relaxation. Outbuildings might include an aisled (or 'basilican') villa for the bailiff, and a less comfortable barn for slaves acquired in local markets or from the Continent. Unwanted slave children born on the estate, especially girls, were killed off much as one might drown a litter of kittens. A villa excavated at Hambleden in Buckinghamshire was found to have its own burial ground containing the corpses of nearly 100 new-born babies. It was simpler to replace slaves than rear them.

A reconstruction of Little Woodbury farmstead on Salisbury Plain

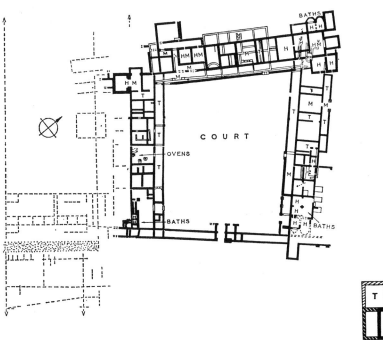

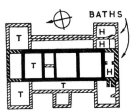

Right : Plan of a winged corridor villa at Hambleden, Buckinghamshire, with later additions including a bath suite. 'T' indicates tessellated floors, 'H' a hypocaust. Left : The elaborate villa which developed over the years at North Leigh, Oxfordshire, surrounding a spacious courtyard. 'M' indicates mosaic pavements.

Reconstruction of an early fourth-century dining-room.

One of the animals under the spell of Orpheus's lyre . The Orpheus mosaic pavement at Woodchester, Gloucestershire.

A nymph swims about the central roundel, also from the Woodchester mosaic pavement.

Even before the conquest, few farmers would have been so incompetent as to site their establishments far from a good water supply. Streams and springs were already tapped to channel water into fields and buildings, and the invaders introduced new applications of this. Every Romano-British villa owner or tenant with any pretensions to gentility had to have a bath-house in one wing of his house or in a separate block. This was no mere cold tub but a suite of rooms offering cold, warm, and hot facilities. Hot water and steam were supplied through a hypocaust system in which a furnace stoked from outside fed hot air under the floors and through wall ducts. A similar technique was employed in kilns for drying corn.

Temples and shrines, large and small, were a feature of town and country life. Strict and dictatorial in so many ways, the Romans were remarkably tolerant of religions differing from their own. Indeed, they amiably adopted several minor deities alongside their official cult. From time to time there

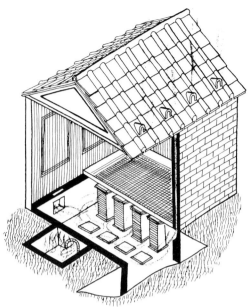

Diagram of a hypocaust, showing the circulation of warm air from a furnace around the supports of a tessellated floor.

The under-floor construction of a hypocaust at Chedworth villa, Gloucestershire.

A gilt-bronze head of the goddess Minerva found in 1727 at Bath, where her cult was linked with that of the Celtic goddess Sulis.

was persecution of adherents to certain creeds deemed to be too subversive or exclusive, such as Judaism and Christianity, but on the whole a great deal of spiritual latitude was allowed. Provided that formal respect was shown to the state-approved trinity of Jupiter, Juno and Minerva, and also to the cult of imperial divinity during the lifetime of those emperors who chose to claim it, other personal and tribal gods were allowed their place. The widely-travelled Roman legions acquired many deities along the way. Mithras became a special favourite

and was imported into Britain: Persian symbol of light and wisdom, he appealed strongly to the army, who may have felt intuitive sympathy for the Mithraic ceremony of blood baptism known as the Taurobolium. Initiatory rites, which included confinement in a pit above which a fire was lit to test the novice's powers of endurance, bore hints of later Masonic ritual. Many features also had something in common with Christianity, which may have accounted for the jealous proscription of the cult and the ravaging of its temples when the Christians, once themselves persecuted, were in a position to inflict their own dogmas throughout the Empire.

Druid sacrificial ceremonies were detested by the Romans, and after stamping them out on the mainland they ruthlessly obliterated the last vestiges in England and Wales. Apart from this, Celtic beliefs relating to the forces of nature were not too different from their own. At Bath a local deity was agreeably combined with a Roman one to create Sulis-Minerva. In the north, Brigantia was elevated to major cult status with additional Roman trappings such as Minerva's spear and shield, and the wings of Victory. At Lanchester in County Durham a local goddess named Garmangarbis was worshipped.

Army barracks had their individual shrines, as did villas and town houses. Tribal centres might install a larger building with a central chamber surrounded by a colonnade, not for the use of a congregation as we know it but for small-scale seasonal observances. There was no equivalent of a church graveyard for interment of the faithful: Roman law forbade burials, other than those of children, within town limits, so cemeteries were located beside highways outside the perimeter.

Only in a few major cities were the temples of any considerable size, and even then they existed for show rather than communal use. One of the most impressive must have been that devoted to the worship of 'Divis Claudius' – Claudius the God – erected around an Altar of Eternal Dominion in the capital of Rome's Britannic province. Its grandiloquence, which aroused cynical comment even in Rome, affirmed the imperial determination to remain in possession of this land, and also Claudius's determination to supplant the Celtic war-god Camulos in Camulodunum.

The huge edifice was not, however, destined for its boasted eternity, and the town was not destined to remain the capital of the province. Colchester in fact was fated to provide early and bloody evidence that any idea of cajoling native chieftains into placid collaboration with benevolent Roman overseers was not going to work all that smoothly.

Romanized relief of Brigantia, with Minerva's spear and the wings of Victory.

Mithras slaying the bull, a marble relief found near the temple of Mithras, Walbrook.

Part of the London city wall in the public garden which was once St Alphage churchyard, off Wood Street.

THE FIRST TOWNSHIPS

UNTIL the Romans imposed their own customs on the populace there had never been what could truly be described as towns in Britain. The tribal *oppida*, no matter how large, were rarely more than clumps of huts within protective dykes and ramparts. The newcomers had little time for ramshackle dwellings or ramshackle administration. Essentially they were city dwellers: their very concept of civilization implied civic laws and standards of living to which all barbarians should be converted.

Upland and border regions remained for a considerable time subject to direct military government, but in the more settled lowland areas some autonomy was encouraged provided it could contribute the taxes in cash and kind which the imperial exchequer demanded. The country was divided up into cantons roughly corresponding to those previously dominated by the relevant tribes, though batches of lesser groups were combined, whether they liked it or not, into larger organizations. Such a local government area was known as a *civitas* with, as it were, its own county town to house tribal magistrates and magnates. Legal and financial officers were appointed from the well-to-do with certain property qualifications. Names of these centres usually incorporated the names of the tribes concerned: Ratae Coritanorum (Leicester) was the capital of the Coritani, Corinium Dobunnorum (Cirencester) the capital of the Dobunni, and the Dumnonii came under Isca Dumnoniorum (Exeter).

The formal plan of any reasonably sized town employed a grid system of streets enclosing blocks of houses, shops and public buildings. In spite of destruction and urban redevelopment over the centuries, these regular patterns can still be identified in the street layout of some of our old established towns and cities. Even the foundations of dwelling houses, temples and public baths show up now and then during site clearance for a modern building project.

Often a craftsman or dealer would, then as now, 'live over the shop' or behind it. His work and display premises faced the street, sometimes in the form of an open stall with shutters which went up at the close of day. Living accommodation might be simple, within a timber-framed house, but if he prospered he would introduce stone, concrete or even mosaic flooring, and decorate his walls with painted plaster. Wealthier merchants and civic dignitaries favoured the fashionable area around the forum, an open central space flanked by colonnades, market hall, and council offices.

As well as the bath suites which private individuals installed in their homes there were public baths, always a popular rendezvous for exercise and conversation. Once inside, the bather had the run of a *palaestra* or exercise yard, followed by an *apodyterium* or disrobing room with lockers, and then the sequence of baths: the *frigidarium*, a cold bath; a *tepidarium* or warm room; and the *caldarium*, a hot room, followed by a sweating chamber similar to a

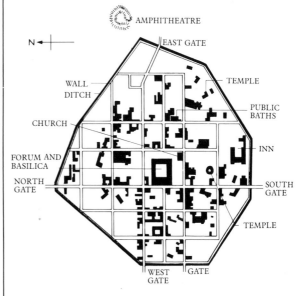

A plan of Silchester. The outline of the city walls is still visible (see illustration on page 59).

A bather's strigil, *or scraper, and oil pot.*

Alma-Tadema's late Victorian painting shows a bather holding a strigil *and, more fancifully, an ostrich feather.*

An oil lamp with a design of women at the baths.

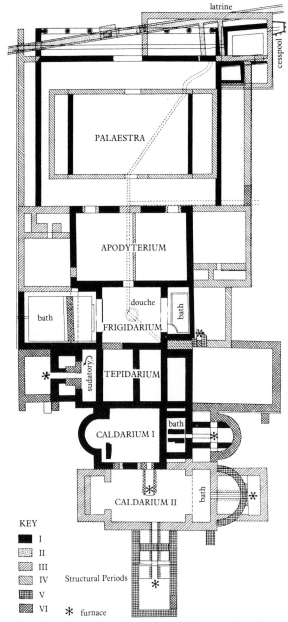

The volume of water required for an urban complex presented more problems than that needed for farmland, but most places managed to install aqueducts or dykes from neighbouring rivers and streams. Lincoln relied on a pipeline from a spring later known as Roaring Meg, and like other towns had timber and lead pipes following the line of its streets. Also in Lincoln, and in several other towns, there were stone sewers below the streets, fed by smaller waste pipes from shops and houses.

Gossip and physical recreation in the bath-house were not the only sources of communal entertainment. Theatres and amphitheatres provided drama, singing, and a setting for religious festivals. No circus of the characteristic Roman pattern has yet been unearthed in this country, but gladiatorial contests and animal baiting were to be found in many an oval amphitheatre with tiers of seating for a large audience.

As well as grouping tribes into specified administrative zones, the new overlords introduced two other forms of township with special privileges. One was the *municipium*, whose inhabitants had a status almost equal to that of full Roman citizens and were allowed wide freedom to run their own affairs. Verulamium (St Albans), which had been the capital of the Catuvellauni before Cunobelinus transferred to Colchester, was the first and only place in Britain to be granted this distinction. The other type was the *colonia*, a settlement for army veterans entitled to housing and a grant of land. With every reason to be grateful to their one-time employers, they provided a nucleus of loyal reservists in the *colonia* if the need arose. There were four such settlements: the first was at Colchester, followed by two more at Lincoln and Gloucester, and later at York.

The original Belgic fortress at Camulodunum covered an area of about 12 square miles (3,096 ha) between the river Colne and what has come to be known as the Roman River. The A12 and roads heading west and south-west from Colchester town centre cut across the site at Lexden and Gosbeck's Farm. A triple line of dykes defended this western flank, deep gashes of which can still be found. An impressive remnant known as Lexden Earthworks is in the care of the Department of the Environment and can be visited at any time. The tumulus beside Fitzwalter Road which was opened in 1924 contained such plentiful treasure that some believe it can only have been the burial hoard of Cunobelinus

A plan of Silchester public baths, which were in use from the first century AD until the decline of the city in the fourth century.

Turkish bath or sauna, and a final cold plunge for those of tough calibre. Soap was unknown. Dirt sweated out was scraped away by the bather, his slave, or a bath attendant, with a strigil – a curved blade with an oiled edge – and was often followed by a massage with oil and perfume. Swimming baths were found only at spas such as Aquae Sulis (Bath) and Aquae Arnemetiae (Buxton), and a wayward example at Viroconium Cornoviorum (Wroxeter).

himself, and Belgic huts from his period were found near Sheepen Farm when the by-pass was being built.

A few years after the storming of these ramparts by Claudius's legions, the veterans' *colonia* of about 100 acres (41 ha) was established to the east of the native settlement, on rising ground with good agricultural tracts below. Quays were built to deal with supplies shipped along the Colne. The veterans were happy with their homes and plots of land; and priests of the massive temple of Claudius were happy with the riches and privileges accruing to them. Local Britons, especially those whose dwellings and land had been commandeered for the benefit of the time-served soldiers, were far from happy. Seizing far more than had been officially allocated, the colonists offered the dispossessed natives labouring work which made virtual slaves of them. The priests battened on them. One of Rome's own historians, Tacitus, admits that the temple was 'a blatant bastion of alien rule' and that its priests used every pretext to 'drain the country dry'.

In AD 48 the governor Ostorius Scapula, anxious to guard against revolt to his rear while he launched a campaign into Wales, ordered that all natives in the province, even those in supposedly favoured minor kingdoms, should be disarmed. This was indignantly resisted by some, above all by the Iceni of Norfolk and Suffolk. A force of auxiliaries sent to implement the measure brought the Iceni to heel at a battle thought to have taken place somewhere near Cambridge. Bad feeling over this humiliation remained. But there was worse humiliation to come in AD 60.

The new governor of the province, Suetonius Paulinus, was engaged like his predecessors with the troublesome question of Wales. Determined to destroy the hated Druids, who had been driven to take refuge on the isle of Mona (Anglesey), he took the cream of his fighting men with him and left the rest of the country inadequately defended. At the same time the imperial procurator Catus Decianus was enraging the client kings by demanding immediate repayment, with heavy interest, of loans and subsidies which had been given them to ensure their cooperation. His worst excesses were directed against the Iceni. Their king Prasutagus had been granted virtual independence, and hoped at his death to preserve this for his two daughters by nominating the emperor joint heir with them to the kingdom. Nero's representative paid no heed to the terms of this bequest, but pressed for the clearance of substantial 'debts'. When the widowed queen, Boudicca (Boadicea), protested she was flogged, her two daughters were raped on Catus's orders, and all Icenian possessions were sequestered.

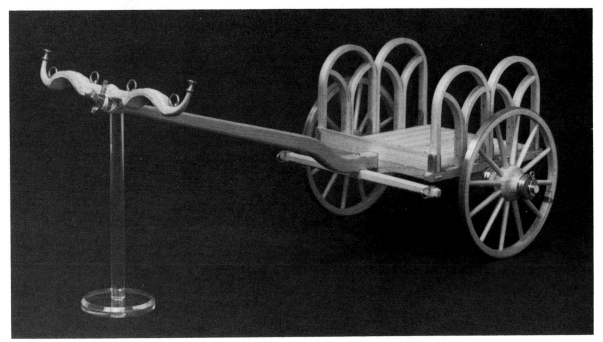

Based on remains from an Anglesey bog, this model of a lightweight chariot shows the type which both the Druid defenders and Boudicca's rebels would have used against the legionaries.

In a rage Boudicca rallied not only the Iceni but the Trinovantes who had been evicted to make way for colonists. In vengeful alliance they descended on Colchester. The town had been only lightly fortified: there were no walls, no properly organized defences. On the approach of the rebel horde a statue of Victory in the town crashed from its plinth, and apprehensive townsfolk observed that it fell with its back to the enemy as if in cowardly flight. Catus Decianus was appealed to for help in the absence of the governor, but sent only a handful of troops to aid the poorly armed garrison. When the tribesmen fell upon the place these defenders were driven for shelter into the temple of Claudius, which was stormed and demolished after a two-day siege. A detachment of the Ninth Legion hurriedly sent to the rescue from Lincoln, or possibly Longthorpe in Cambridgeshire, was also butchered by the Britons. When the news reached Catus Decianus he fled in disgrace to Gaul.

Victorious Boudicca ordered the burning of the town after her followers had grabbed as much loot as they could find. Then she turned her attention to the growing supply and trade centre of Londinium (London) which had expanded around the important Thames crossing. Notified of the insurrection, Suetonius Paulinus rushed cavalry units ahead of his infantry in a dash from the west. On reaching London he decided that his forces were unsufficient for a decisive battle, and after evacuating as many of the inhabitants as possible he withdrew and left the town to its fate. London and St Albans suffered in the same way as Colchester: indiscriminate massacre, plundering, and burning. Only when all available reinforcements had been mustered could he set out in earnest to corner the queen and her warriors. Their confrontation took place somewhere in the Midlands, possibly by Watling Street in the neighbourhood of Towcester or Atherstone in Northamptonshire.

According to Tacitus, before battle was joined Boudicca and her daughters drove in their chariot around their troops so that she could exhort them in language eerily prophetic of Queen Elizabeth's words at the time of the Spanish Armada:

We British are used to women commanders in war. I am descended from mighty men. ... Consider how many of you are fighting, and why! Then will you win this battle or perish. That is what I, a woman, intend to do. Let the men live in slavery if they will!

The Colchester Vase, also known as The Gladiator Vase because of its relief figures of a gladiatorial contest.

In spite of these brave words the tide of war turned against the rebels. Roman regulars and auxiliaries pitted remorseless and tightly disciplined methods and weapon power against a tumultuous rabble; and won. When Boudicca saw that defeat could not be averted she took poison rather than suffer further indignities at Roman hands. Her body, like that of King Arthur, has many legendary burial sites – in her case, mainly in the Midlands and East Anglia – but no solid evidence to authenticate any of them.

Paulinus set about rounding up the scattered rebels, to whom he showed no mercy. His punitive programme did not slacken until a new procurator was sent to replace the one who had contributed so much to the damage, and at once appealed direct to Nero for clemency so that order and decency could be restored to the province. Himself the son of a Gaul who had risen to high office in the imperial service, Julius Alpinus Classicianus may have felt covert sympathy for the downtrodden natives of a conquered land. Nero sent one of his favourite freedmen to check on the procurator's report, agreed with it, replaced Suetonius Paulinus, and opened the way to a relaxation of the savage reprisals.

All three razed towns were rebuilt and, despite

hopes of future harmony, prudently supplied with better defences; though St Albans seems to have taken a good 10 years to re-establish itself, by which time London was asserting its supremacy in the province.

Such remains as can be found above the surface of modern Colchester represent this and later stages. Defensive walls with at least six gateways were added in due course, their circuit still traceable in spite of the gaps and infillings of centuries. Impressive sections are visible in Priory Street and Vineyard Street as well as in the castle park, with remains of a small gateway in Holly Trees Meadow by the park. The remains of a Mithraic temple were excavated behind The Hollytrees local domestic museum between 1927 and 1929.

The castle, which incorporated a great deal of Roman tile and brickwork, was set by the Normans upon the platform of Claudius's ruined temple. They seem to have been unaware of the existence of vaults beneath this base. Rediscovered in 1683, the vaults can now be visited by the public, and some idea of their lost superstructure may be gained from a fine model of the whole temple in the castle museum. This museum houses one of the largest collection of relics from any one Roman site in the British Isles, including coins and charred remnants from the first *colonia*, and touching personal and domestic objects such as ointment bottles, hairpins, earrings, combs, children's toys, and a baby's terracotta feeding bottle. Among the military tombstones, there is one of a cavalryman trampling down an opponent, and another of the centurion Marcus Favonius Facilis in full uniform.

A model of the temple of Claudius which dominated the Colchester forum. It was so grandiose that even the Romans themselves mocked it.

Toys found within a child's grave in Lexden tumulus on the outskirts of Colchester.

This tombstone was gratefully erected by two freedmen of Marcus Favonius Facilis, a centurion of the Twentieth Legion at Colchester, showing him with a vine-staff, virtually a 'swagger-stick' indicative of his rank.

A head of Claudius, probably thrown into the river Alde by a fleeing Icenian, and rediscovered in 1907.

A reconstruction that can be more rewardingly compared with its original is the museum's model of the Balkerne Gate. Through this gate ran the highway to and from London, on the line of the present High Street, past the George Hotel in whose basement bar is exhibited the scorched outline of one of the houses burnt by Boudicca. Jauntily topped by a public house, the surviving two arches of the gateway are the truncated remains of a large structure with two openings for traffic and narrower pedestrian arches to either side, guarded by D-shaped bastions. Downhill there runs a solid chunk of wall. The model shows the full extent of the portal, complete with convincing figures of the period.

The modern Mercury Theatre, a few steps within the Balkerne Gate, carries above it a facsimile of the small bronze statue of Mercury found in temple excavations at Gosbeck's Farm. Not far from the temple there was also a theatre, excavated in 1967. Much further away, across the Suffolk border, there reappeared a bronze head of Claudius which must have been looted from Colchester by one of Boudicca's supporters and then thrown away from fear of retribution, to lie in the river Alde until 1907. It was fished out by a boy who whitewashed it and hung it outside his cottage until it was bought from him for five shillings – later to be acquired by the British Museum for considerably more than that.

A reconstruction of the Balkerne Gate in Colchester's west wall, a monumental arch later converted into a double gateway with smaller arches for pedestrians.

A segment of stone and tile wall at Verulamium, on the outskirts of St Albans.

Just as the Romans had placed their Colchester settlement slightly away from the conquered *oppidum*, so they ordained a new Verulamium at what came to be St Albans. The Belgic site had been in Prae Wood, about a mile east of the present abbey church. Now it was shifted into a purpose-built *municipium* beside the Watling Street highway, which during post-Boudiccan reconstruction was straddled by a triumphal arch whose foundations are still distinguishable.

After the subjugation of the Iceni the defences were strengthened by a rampart and ditch. Early in the second century two miles (3.2 km) of stone wall and bastions were added, reinforced by guardhouses at every gateway. One can get a good prospect of wall remains from the bank of the river Ver near the Fighting Cocks Inn. Below St Michael's church is buried a basilican town hall, leaving only one corner marked out in the grass near the cark park. Shop footings scorched during the rebellion adjoin a 1934 excavation which turned out to be the horseshoe-shaped auditorium of a Roman-style theatre as opposed to the more common circular arena of an amphitheatre. Seating on the earthen tiers was backed by a high earthwork formed from spoil dug out during construction.

Within a protective brick shelter is part of a bath suite with mosaic pavement and hypocaust. The tessellations and their surround suffered, as did many wall and roof remains, when Norman monks helped themselves to brick and tile for use in the tower of their abbey.

The abbey is dedicated to St Alban, a third-century legionary who, during persecution of Christians, hid a British priest and by his example was converted to the faith. After helping his mentor to escape he was executed on the hill where the abbey now stands. A decade later the Emperor Constantine was also converted, and ordained the raising of a small shrine on the spot. In Saxon times Offa built a monastery over it, and the Normans contributed a more spacious building in 1077.

The road on which Verulamium stood was one of the most important in the province. A posting

The open-air theatre at Verulamium, with turf

banks to support seating around the open stage.

station was set between it and Londinium at Sulloniacae (Brockley Hill), from which height the road-builders' south-eastern sighting had taken them straight down into what is now the Edgware Road. At first only a secondary supply port and a market for merchants of mainly British origin, London profited from the shift of emphasis after Boudicca's defeat. The first London Bridge, close to the span of its famous successors, was basically part of a military transport route from Richborough and other harbours on the Channel coast; but an energetic business community soon dug itself in on the north bank. Although there appears to have been no Celtic settlement of any consequence here before the Romans arrived, the name of London is itself Celtic – perhaps derived from the name of a farm or a tribal magnate – and was duly Latinized into Londinium.

Boudicca had left the port devastated. During the digging of modern foundations within the City many a level of scorched clay or pottery has been revealed. Another burnt stratum was added to this early in the second century when an accidental fire raged through streets and buildings, after which the place was rebuilt yet again. An abundant source of relics from various phases has been the bed of the Walbrook stream, navigable in Roman and medieval times but now channelled through a main

Skulls from the bed of the Walbrook stream, London.

sewer. Skulls hereabouts may have been those of Londoners slaughtered by the Iceni. The frequent discovery of writing tablets, on which messages or mathematical calculations were cut by a stylus into wax on a wooden backing, suggests that the neighbourhood was already establishing its tradition as a centre for accountants, ledger clerks, usurers, and other such scribblers. Coins, tools, brooches, amulets and clay figures of Venus were probably votive offerings cast into the stream. Certainly there were several shrines in the vicinity.

Most impressive of such religious buildings was the basilican temple of Mithras on the east bank of the Walbrook. Few of us who commuted in and out of Cannon Street station in 1954 will forget the excitement as layer after layer was stripped away to show the full proportions of the Mithraeum, some 60 ft long and 20 ft wide (18.2 by 6 m). Its appearance was not unlike that of a simple Christian church, containing a nave divided by columns from two side aisles. At the west end was a sanctuary within a rounded apse. But the presiding deities were not Christian: marble effigies included heads of Mithras wearing the Phrygian cap always associated with him, of the Egyptian god Serapis whose cult had been introduced to Rome along with that of Isis; and Minerva for once shown without her helmet. A sculpted group belonging to a late stage of the temple's history – which ran from the end of the first century until the middle of the fourth – shows Bacchus in the company of the wine-bibbing satyr Silenus and others, with a cordial inscription recommending wine as 'life to wandering men'.

After records had been prepared of the Mithraeum, and all its treasures removed, the office block of Bucklersbury House rose above the sacred enclosure; but a ground plan formed by material salvaged from the temple is preserved in a base outside the adjoining Temple Court.

Mosaic of a sea-god, once part of a Verulamium floor.

Ground plan of the Walbrook temple of Mithras, using original stones from the site, now embedded outside Temple Court, Queen Victoria Street.

A marble group from the Mithraeum, showing Bacchus and companions.

A marble head of Mithras found in the Mithraeum, wearing the Phrygian cap always associated with him.

A marble head of Serapis from the Mithraeum. An Egyptian god adopted by the Romans in the middle of the second century, he was associated with licentious rites and finally proscribed by the Senate.

A conjectural aerial view of London's city wall in course of construction.

Under Cannon Street station lie the foundations of a great palace, and a forum fronting a basilican town hall has been overlaid by Leadenhall Market and bisected by Gracechurch Street. A fine mosaic from Leadenhall Street was removed to the British Museum.

With its quays and commerce and easy access to the Continent by means of traffic up and down the Thames, London was well set to replace Colchester as the seat of Roman government. Shops and houses destroyed by Boudicca, and others deemed unworthy of the new capital, gave way to civic and commercial buildings on a grander scale. A tileworks was founded to manufacture material for the new developments, and all of its products were stamped P.P.BR.LON. to attest the authority of the procurator of the Province of Britain at Londinium. Other materials could be shipped from abroad or from the countryside to wooden riverside wharves, including marble from Italy and ragstone from Kent. One load of ragstone was discovered in 1962 in a sunken barge near Blackfriars, estimated to have been commissioned around AD 89 because a coin of

that date was found in the mast instep, a good luck ritual still observed by boatbuilders. At Billingsgate during 1982 and early 1983 archaeologists from the Museum of London strove to record and salvage as much as possible from timbered Roman and Saxon quays before concrete and glass obscured them forever.

A stone fort just outside the north-west corner of the city probably came into being as barracks for the resident military governor's staff and personal escort when London was acknowledged as provincial capital. Foundations of a corner turret and an intermediate turret, together with accompanying walls, were unearthed in 1956 in Noble Street. Part of the west gate is preserved below the dual carriageway of London Wall.

At the end of the second century it was decided to enclose the whole city within one formidable wall. This may have been undertaken because of signs that the long tranquillity of the south-eastern sector of the province was endangered by disputes within the Roman hierarchy. After the assassination of two emperors the governor of Britain, Clodius Albinus,

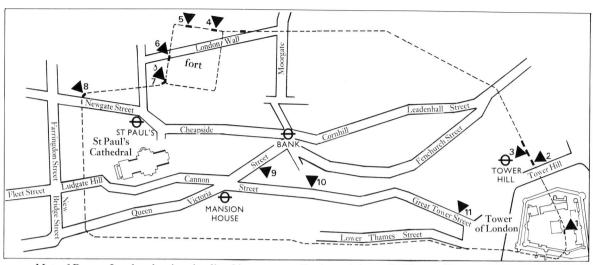

Map of Roman London showing sites listed in gazetteer. Sections of city wall: Tower of London (1) Wakefield Gardens (2) Cooper's Row (3) St Alphage churchyard (4) St Giles Cripplegate churchyard (5). West gate of fort (6). Fort foundations and turret (7). Bastion (8). Mithraeum (9). London Stone (10). Tessellated floor (11).

The London Stone in Cannon Street, thought to have been the milliarium from which distances from London were measured. It originally stood on the other side of the street, but was moved in 1798 to be inset in the wall of St Swithun's church, which was demolished in 1962 and replaced by the Bank of China.

declared himself rightful heir to the imperial throne and drained the country of troops to support him on the Continent. He lost out on his venture and was killed in 197. Also he came close to losing Britain for the Empire. Old antagonists swarmed down from the north to harass the Romanized tribes or win them over. Just as London in later years was to panic at rumours of the approach of Bonnie Prince Charlie, so there were earlier apprehensions about the future of the Romano-British capital.

The wall incorporated the existing fort and made use of its walls, thereby producing from their different alignments a couple of awkward angles untypical of the usual squared-up Roman construction. The western spread of the wall carried it from the fort through Aldersgate to Newgate, and then it turned straight down to the river near Blackfriars. Eastwards it ran to Bishopsgate, turned towards Aldgate, and reached the river right through the site of the Tower of London. Although much of our past was wantonly destroyed by Victorian and other developers, the designers of the 1909 General Post Office at St Martin's-le-Grand had the taste and foresight to preserve an impressive section of the wall and one of its bastions in the fabric of their building.

A century or more later a riverside wall was added, possibly against the threat of Saxon pirates whose raids were striking up-river and deeper into the country. And at some stage, perhaps to stiffen the backbone of the populace and give them cause for pride, London was elevated above all other

An impression by Alan Sorrell of the public bath-house known to have existed by Cheapside, London.

towns in the province by the designation of Augusta – the majestic – and introduced this on coins minted here.

It is fascinating to speculate as to how much of Roman London may be embalmed several layers below our own superimposed city. Even before the discovery of the Bucklersbury Mithraeum in our own time a mosaic pavement was exposed in Bucklersbury and visited by curious crowds during the laying of Queen Victoria Street in 1869. Private bath-houses have shown up when foundations were dug for office blocks. Some conscientious contractors allow time for archaeologists to study their finds before proceeding; but delays are expensive, and one suspects that many an unveiled treasure is hastily covered over again. It is hard to blame construction companies: like most great cities, London rests on many different strata of history, and there is no way in which Roman, Norman, medieval and Georgian features can be meticulously preserved cheek by jowl – or even one on top of the other. Nevertheless it is good to attempt the main-

tenance of at least the skeleton of our past, to compare one pattern with its successor, and be always conscious that under modern pavements lie the paths and alleys and pavements of a quite different kind and different era, echoing to the tread of our forbears.

When we drive out of London from Newgate through Notting Hill and on to Staines we are following in the steps of legionaries and traders on the busy thoroughfare to Silchester and on along the Port Way to Old Sarum. Our A5 is largely Watling Street. Heading north from Bishopsgate through Shoreditch and Edmonton to Ware we use stretches of Ermine Street, which continues through Godmanchester and Royston to join the A1 for some miles before swinging off to Lincoln. If we fancy accompanying Chaucer's Canterbury pilgrims in spirit or in a car from the southern end of London Bridge we shall not stray far from another important section of Watling Street.

Also at London Bridge there begins the route to a loyal client king's home and harbour at Chichester.

The road network linking civitas capitals and other major towns in the Roman province.

PLACES TO VISIT

National grid references are supplied in the gazetteer sections for remoter sites so that they can be pinpointed on the Ordnance Survey Scale 1:50 000 maps. The reference below for Lexden Dyke, for example, is TL 963245. The letters TL identify the 100 km square in which the site falls. Along the top of the map are numbers at 1 km intervals called eastings, and at the sides are similar numbers called northings. In this case find the easting 96 and move beyond it to 0.3 km. Then find the northing 24 and move up a further 0.5 km. The site is where the easting and the northing cross.

Colchester, Essex
Balkerne Gate, Balkerne Hill. Castle museum with large Roman collections and Claudius's temple vaults. Lexden Dyke, TL 963245, off A1124 2 miles (3.2 km) W of town centre.

London
Fort foundations and turrets, Noble Street, EC2.

West gate of fort, London Wall, EC2 (group admission only, by prior arrangement with Museum of London).

Sections of city wall near St Giles Cripplegate churchyard, EC2; Cooper's Row, EC3; St Alphage churchyard, EC2, Wood Street, EC2; Wakefield Gardens, Trinity Place, EC3; and Tower of London. Bastion and section of wall in GPO, St Martin's-le-Grand, EC1 (admission by application to the Postmaster Controller).

London Stone, milestone in Bank of China façade, Cannon Street, EC4.

Ground plan of Mithraeum, Temple Court, Queen Victoria Street, EC4.

Tessellated floor, All Hallows Barking Church, EC3 (on application to the verger).

Roman collections in the British Museum, Great Russell Street, WC1; and Museum of London, London Wall, EC2.

St Albans, Hertfordshire
Public park on NW outskirts with theatre, mosaic, hypocaust, museum, and surviving walls of Verulamium.

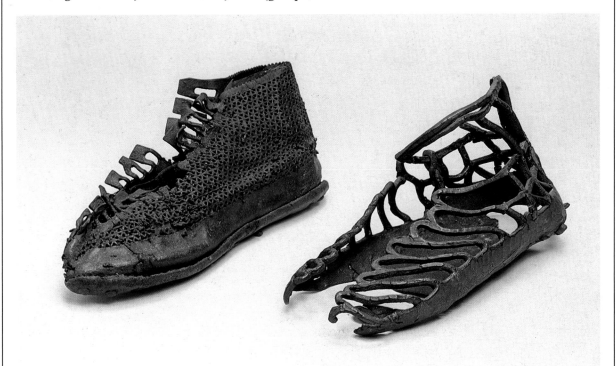

Roman leather shoes found in London. Both have loops through which shoelaces would have been threaded.

The ring of beeches planted on Chanctonbury Hill in 1760 shelters an Iron Age site and a Romano-British temple.

SOUTH AND SOUTH-EAST

AMONG the tribes which had welcomed the coming of the legions was that of the Regni or Regnenses, who had already forged strong ties with Rome. Partly under the sway of the more powerful Atrebates of Berkshire and Hampshire, they were united with them in mutual anger against the despotic Catuvellauni. The exiled king of the Atrebates, Verica, was one of those supplicants whose direct personal appeals to Claudius helped spark off the Roman expedition.

We cannot be sure whether or not Verica was restored to his kingdom, but if so he could not have reigned for long, since the acknowledged client king soon after the invasion was Cogidubnus. The high esteem in which this ruler came to be held is shown in the Latin inscription of a stone set into the Council House wall in North Street, Chichester. Dug up from a street corner in 1723 and kept until 1907 in a garden pavilion at Goodwood, this dedicates a temple to Neptune and Minerva

on behalf of the safety of the Divine House on the authority of Tiberius Claudius Cogidubnus, King and Legate of Augustus in Britain, by the Gild of artificers and its associate members from their own contributions.

The near-divine title of 'Augustus' had been bestowed on the first Roman emperor by the Senate as an expression of veneration and was gladly adopted by most of his imperial successors, including Claudius. The obeisance towards the god of the sea and the goddess of arts and crafts may indicate that the guild concerned was that of local shipyard workers and dockers. As late as AD 97 Cogidubnus was recorded by Tacitus as displaying 'unswerving loyalty down to our own times'; and the historian wryly adds that this is in line with 'the long-established Roman practice of employing even kings to make slaves of others'.

Those who favour the theory of a tripartite attack by Aulus Plautius's invasion fleet have suggested Itchenor, Hayling Island, or West Wittering on the Selsey peninsula as likely debarkation points. Whatever doubts there may be about this, there can be no doubt that the Romans promptly made Chichester the capital of a *civitas* as Noviomagus Regnensium, while the Atrebates were shifted back where they had come from, with a capital at Calleva Atrebatum (Silchester).

Streets in the centre of modern Chichester follow the Roman plan fairly closely, and the medieval walls rest on verifiably Roman foundations. The forum and basilica were traditionally placed near the intersection of the main east–west and north–south roads within a town, and so it was here: they are known to lie buried below the cathedral, which stands just beyond the crossroads. An amphitheatre discovered in 1935 was built over again. In 1972 greater respect was shown to the past. An architect watching the sinking of foundations for a development on Eastgate Square was puzzled by a mixture of mortar and sandstone which the mechanical digger was beginning to churn up, and, to the credit of the site owners, work was stopped until archaeological investigation could be carried out on what proved to be a fourth-century Roman bastion of the east gate through which Stane Street entered the city.

At regular intervals beside this road to London were set posting stations, such as those identified at Hardham and Alfoldean. It was predictable that wealthy Romano-British farmers would be glad to

The laudatory inscription linking Neptune and Minerva with the unusually honoured Cogidubnus.

The line of Stane Street, the highway from Chichester to London, diagonally across the picture.

Model of Fishbourne palace as it probably looked about 75 AD, on the edge of what was then a deep-water anchorage.

connect their villas to such a route, and perhaps build new ones. There were some in the Pulborough and Wiggonholt area, but the most substantial remains, under the lee of the South Downs, are those at Bignor.

In 1811 a plough dislodged a large stone to reveal part of a mosaic of dancing girls. The landowner and a colleague spent eight years digging and sifting through the earth, bit by bit laying bare the floors of a spacious house that had been added to and improved between the second and fourth centuries. In the preserved range of the west wing, different shades of asphalt have been laid to mark successive stages of development. There were living-rooms, bathrooms, and an extensive central heating system. Until the middle of our own century the source of water for this puzzled experts, but then pipe trenches were found running north towards a stream bed from which supplies must have been pumped into cisterns and then gravity-fed to the estate.

The most appealing features of the Bignor villa are its mosaic floors, testifying to the occupants' profits from large-scale sheep ranching on the Downs, and to their admirable taste.

At Bignor the discovery of the dancing girls led on to a further discovery in the same room of a depiction of Jupiter's eagle carrying off Ganymede, so beautifully executed as to appear three-dimensional. Other rooms feature geometrical mosaics, a study of bleak winter that is the sole survivor of what was surely a seasonal sequence,

and, most sensuously lovely of all, a head of Venus composed of unusually small stones, with an accompanying panel of gladiators attired as rather cuddly winged cupids.

Luxurious as this gentleman farmer's house may have been, it is outshone by a veritable palace on the outskirts of Chichester. At Fishbourne the main Portsmouth road cuts across what can only have been the residence of that favoured client king, Cogidubnus. Coins and shards of pottery had often turned up in the neighbourhood, and even a section of tessellated pavement; but it was not until 1960 that a workman laying a water main came upon rubble which hinted at the existence of something really distinctive. The local archaeological society embarked on several years of painstaking excavation to establish the conformation of a great building with enclosed formal gardens irrigated by ceramic water conduits, a spacious courtyard, colonnades, bath houses, a guest wing, and a regal audience chamber. We do not know how many mosaic floors and brightly plastered walls have been crushed under the roads and dwellings of later generations, but sheltered within modern glass and airy roofing there survive representations of a cupid riding on a dolphin in a surround of fabulous sea beasts, and a geometrical teaser calculated to trick the eye of the beholder. Deeper still were traces of what must have been naval warehouses from the earliest days of the invasion, and a less grandiose house from which the palace was eventually expanded.

MOSAICS

A mosaic pavement below Butcher Lane in Canterbury, Kent.

Mosaic designs, an invention of the ancient Greeks, were produced by sinking pieces of coloured stone or glass into a cement bed. In the course of time the inset pieces, known as *tesserae*, were usually standardized into small cubes which could be employed in black-and-white geometrical patterns or in coloured representations of gods, animals, and mythical monsters against stylized backgrounds. Once the fashion had caught on, schools of mosaicists sprang up in Britain, at first copying Continental models and then refining their own techniques. Products of a Cirencester workshop can be recognized at Chedworth and Woodchester villas, among others; Dorchester was highly esteemed; and there were cruder attempts in the north of the province, where Rudston villa housed some distorted and blundering experiments, which are now on show in Hull Museum.

The mosaic pavement at Woodchester, Gloucestershire, is the largest yet discovered north of the Alps. A modern copy for public viewing has been constructed at the Tabernacle Church, Wotton-under-Edge.

A dolphin from one of the mosaic floors at Bignor villa, Sussex.

A reconstruction of a mosaicist's workshop, with tools and cubes of stone and pottery to form the patterns.

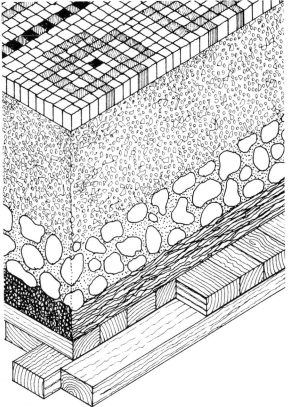

The cubes or tesserae *had to be laid evenly on a firm cement of mortar and broken pottery, usually supported by a wooden plank base.*

A second-century mosaic in what came to be the main room at Fishbourne, showing a cupid riding on a dolphin.

After the death of Cogidubnus there is no record of any influential successor, and the palace seems to have been split up into the equivalent of luxury flats. Somewhere around AD 280 a serious fire destroyed most of the complex, which was not restored and never again inhabited. Instead, local pilferers picked their way through shattered tiles, charred rafters and broken glass and pottery to collect building material for their own use.

What may have been a suburban adjunct of Fishbourne palace, or part of a group of living quarters and offices for military and naval supervisors, was a building discovered south of the road near Bosham station; and not far from it a hollow with tiers of seats could have served as an amphitheatre. Beside the same road was found a marble head thought to depict Germanicus, grandson of Augustus. In Bosham church the bases of Roman columns support the chancel arch, and another sculpted head found here is most likely that of Vespasian, who used the harbour and port as the base for his campaigns further west.

Facilities of other ports in the south and southeast were expanded over the years. Richborough remained the main army supply base, while London flourished as a trading centre, but there were others. The Kentish river Stour was navigable from what was then a wide estuary at Richborough as far as Fordwich, which long after the Romans had gone functioned as terminus for waterborne traffic serving Durovernum Cantiacorum (Canterbury).

Canterbury itself has little of Roman origin to show above ground – apart from the Dane John burial mound and a flicker of red bricks in the walls of St Martin's old church – but it sprawls above a once extensive Romano-British centre. The wall foundations are Roman, and outside on the London and Sturry roads have been found cemeteries of different periods. The regular visitor is treated to happy surprises when new building sites reveal angles of old town houses, a hint of a mosaic, a hypocaust. In 1976 a theatre a good 250 ft (76 m) across with walls 12 ft (3.6 m) thick was found at the junction of Watling Street and St Margaret's Street, but only a corner is now visible within the restaurant which has taken its place. A mosaic and hypocaust are preserved in Butchery Lane. One hopes more will emerge from time to time and that it will not be too unfeelingly re-interred.

Richborough once stood on Tanatus, the Isle of Thanet, separated by the Wantsum channel from the main part of Kent. Its earliest defences consisted of earth ramparts protecting timber warehouses, weapon stores, workshops and barrack blocks. These earthworks erected by the very first troops on this bridgehead can still be seen near the west gate; and at that same gate began the supply route to Canterbury and on beyond it to London.

By AD 85 it was considered that the conquest of the whole country was reasonably secure. In honour of the emperor Domitian and the provincial governor Agricola a marble victory monument was set up at Richborough. It appears to have been a huge four-way arch about 90 ft (28 m) high, visible to all shipping passing up the Wantsum channel, accompanied by marble pillars and bronze statues. At some later stage it was reduced to the dimensions of a lookout post, but material removed from it has been unearthed and is exhibited in the site museum. The remaining base of the paved passage between the arches gives an awe-inspiring notion of the weight it must have been designed to bear. Like its fellows down the east and south-east coasts, the fort was later heavily reinforced by stone walls to resist Saxon pirates and would-be invaders – the story of which is told in the final chapter of this book.

A bedding trench in the gardens at Fishbourne.

The Dover pharos, *or lighthouse, beside the Saxon church of St Mary in the Castle.*

At Dubris (Dover) the original fort and fleet headquarters were built over long ago, to be only briefly exposed again during road-building operations in recent years; but on the eastern hill within the castle stands a *pharos*, or lighthouse, which once had a companion on the western heights of the harbour; and fragments of later fortifications can be seen near the 'painted house' with its coloured wall plaster in New Street.

Anderida (Pevensey), like Richborough, was once closer to the sea than it is now. Even in Norman times, when the Roman emplacement provided a fine bailey for a larger castle complete with a tower keep, ships could still be drawn up close to the massive walls. In the Second World War it was well equipped to play its part again: a 'pill-box' and two machine-gun posts were blended neatly into the stonework.

The most easterly of these 'forts of the Saxon Shore' was Portus Adurni (Portchester) overlooking Portsmouth Harbour and so many phases of naval activity. Once again the Normans were able to use the Roman base for their own castle and square keep. Naval associations have always been close –

Walls and bastions of Pevensey castle, Sussex.

after Dover it was probably the most important anchorage of the Classis Britannica, or British Fleet.

Besides its primary task of transporting troops into the battle zone and mounting regular coastal patrols, the navy had to organize supplies to the occupying forces. Frontier garrisons needed shipments of iron and weapons fashioned from iron. In order to finalize quantities and dispatch schedules it was simpler to give the navy direct responsibility for actual industrial production. This is the soundest explanation of the fact that tiles found on Romano-British workings for iron ore extraction and smelting, such as those at Cranbrook and Crowhurst, are generally stamped CL BR to acknowledge the jurisdiction of the Classis Britannica.

Rich deposits of ore ran from the fringes of Romney Marsh through the Weald of Kent, Sussex and Surrey as far as Haslemere. Today there is farmland where once was thick forest which the Saxons were to call Andredsweald – perhaps a combination of the remembered Roman name of Anderida with the suffix of 'wood' or 'wild'. Iron Age settlers had laid out their encampments well above this dense woodland. Both they and their Roman successors exploited the veins of ore but preferred to operate on the outskirts of the forest, whose trees of course supplied ample fuel for smelting. Under naval urging the workers penetrated further into that reputedly impenetrable wild. Ivan Margary's *Roman Ways in the Weald*, first published in 1948, was a revelation to those who had been taught to think of the Weald in olden times as a trackless jungle warily skirted by successive invaders.

Between 1960 and 1968, excavations near Wadhurst in Sussex disclosed a number of timber buildings, furnaces, and supply roads. Tiles fallen from the sheds carry the CL BR stamp. Archaeologists analysing the specimens estimate that this site alone must have produced at least 10,000 tons of iron during the 100 years of its working life. In 1972 another interesting site at Broadfield, near Crawley, was found to have a battery of over 30 small furnaces.

Cinders and slag were utilized in the construction of roads to supply London with iron products and grain from the South Downs. One section between London and Lewes has been preserved at Holtye

Portchester castle, a key Roman naval base, later the embarkation point for Edward III on his way to victory at Crécy, and Henry V at Agincourt.

This relief shows wine barrels being transported by ship.

near East Grinstead to show the slag surface, complete with ancient wheel marks and what looks like the dip of a shallow ford or 'watersplash'.

We have noted that the Romans forbade burials within city limits. Their cemeteries are found by the roadside. Although interment of dead bodies was not proscribed, cremation was the favoured procedure. One of the greatest collections of funerary urns in this country was found in 1925 at Hassocks, close to the London-to-Brighton railway line and the junction of the Brighton and Hurstpierpoint roads. A Roman road from here in fact marched straight to a link with what is now the A2037 into Shoreham. The discovery of the dead resulted from sand diggings carried out so indiscriminately that much valuable evidence was lost before a discerning eye could inspect what was emerging. Nevertheless a great hoard of Roman cremation urns was found alongside earlier Bronze Age ones, and even some from the subsequent Saxon era. This was a remarkable juxtaposition: Saxons on the whole shunned Roman buildings and cemeteries, and in any case were not in the habit of cremating their dead. Yet here they all were, side by side. The ashes were supplied with the conventional bowls of food and drink, and here and there a coin to pay for their passage across the Styx. Some Samian pottery bowls extracted from the sandpit are kept in the Barbican House Museum at Lewes.

Today the Wealden slopes and certain parts of Hampshire (with East Anglia following suit in recent years) have shown that in spite of pessimistic predictions it is possible to make good wine in England. That the Romans attempted it is almost certain. Imports of wine from Spain, Bordeaux or

Wine barrels of silver fir which were later used to line wells in Silchester.

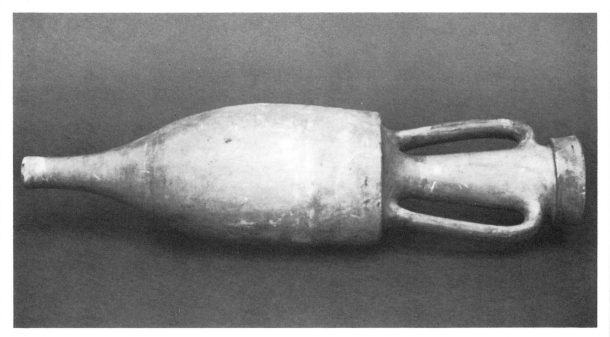

A wine amphora *in red pottery dating from early in the first century, found at Stanmore in Middlesex.*

the homeland were expensive and risked deterioration during the voyage. The emperor Probus's specific grant of permission to Britain in the third century, together with Spain and Gaul, to re-establish its own vineyards after a period of prohibition enforced to safeguard the Italian wine trade surely indicates that possibilities here had already been tested. Fir wine barrels found at Silchester may have been used for incoming shipments; but pips also found there must have been from the pressing of local grapes.

Silchester was the cantonal capital decreed by the provincial legate for the Atrebates. It was founded upon the *oppidum* of Commius, a Belgic chieftain who had at first been an ally of Julius Caesar and then such an enemy that he found it necessary to flee to Britain, announcing his intention of never setting eyes on a Roman again. In spite of this it was his own son Tincommius who, three decades after Caesar's invasion, made placatory gestures to Rome and was soon trading profitably and importing Roman luxuries. His youngest brother Verica was to show more appetite for importing Roman liberators than for their luxuries.

Refashioning the native settlement into the administrative hub of a *civitas* took some 30 years. A large earthwork defining its boundary was later backed by a ditch and another earthen bank. Then in the third century a flint and limestone wall was

added to enclose what was proving to be one of the most spacious cities in the province.

A complete circuit of the wall remains in place, with a small amphitheatre just outside the eastern edge. Within there is now only level farmland with a farmhouse – no Roman villa, this – and a small church. After those great days the city for some reason failed to prosper. Glevum lived on as Gloucester, Venta Belgarum as Winchester, Deva as Chester. Other communities found other destinies. But Silchester, abandoned, was gradually effaced. Excavations of its interior began in 1864 and, with due regard for the needs of the owner and farmer of the land, continued on and off until 1909, after which only limited investigations were allowed in the 1930s and again in the 1960s. What these disinterments revealed was a wonderfully preserved layout of streets, mansions, housing blocks, baths, temples, a forum, and a basilican town hall over 230 ft (70 m) long with two rows of tall Corinthian columns. There was even a small church which might have been pagan but which some students have come to accept as the first identifiable Christian church in this country.

Seven main roads converged on Silchester, among them a main highway from London and one to and from the coast at Southampton. Within the busy triangle formed by the coastline, the Chichester road, and the road through Old Sarum to

Silchester wall near the south gate of the lost city.

The crop markings visible here give a clear impression of buried Silchester within its surviving walls.

A girl flute player bronze, measuring $4\frac{1}{2}$ in (11 cm).

A gilded bronze eagle found in the excavations of the basilica at Silchester.

A geometric mosaic at Rockbourne villa in Hampshire.

The hypocaust at Rockbourne.

Poole was to be found a profusion of villas, many doubtless supplying Silchester with food and exporting the surplus to Gaul.

At Rockbourne, not far from a minor fort on Rockbourne Down, evidence of a large villa was noticed during the Second World War by a farmer trying to dig out a ferret. He came across a number of oyster shells, a common indication of Roman presence since this dish was greatly favoured by the imperial authorities and their imitators. Detailed exploration had to wait, but when undertaken it established the existence of three wings enclosing a courtyard, one of them more than 130 ft (40 m) long, centre of a large sheep or cattle ranch. The north-west range contained a bath suite, and the floors were inlaid with geometric mosaics.

A similar conformation of three wings round a courtyard made up an equally sumptuous residence near Brading on the Isle of Wight. A separate bath-house is to be found in an outbuilding in one corner of the yard. Mosaic pavements include a depiction of Orpheus with his lyre, and one of a man with the head of a cock engaged in what looks like a symbolic rite connected with Eleusinian mysteries of seasonal death and rebirth.

The Isle of Wight was one of the early successes in Vespasian's westward thrust from his Chichester supply base. It is recorded that at the head of the Second Legion he subdued 20 hill-forts and two major tribes in 30 battles. Operations in the coastal lowlands may have been comparatively straightforward. The real challenge came when he found himself up against more towering strongholds and more pugnacious tribesmen, so that even when defeated their territories had to be garrisoned for many years.

PLACES TO VISIT

Bignor, Sussex
North wing of villa, part of baths, mosaics. Site museum. SU 988147, off A285 10 miles (16 km) NE of Chichester.

Bosham, Sussex
Chancel arch of church on Roman pillars. SU 804038, on unclassified road off A27 3 miles (4.8 km) W of Chichester.

Brading, Isle of Wight
Villa rooms, mosaics, display of finds from excavations. SZ 599853, off A3055 S of Brading.

Canterbury, Kent
Mosaic pavement and hypocaust, Butchery Lane. Finds from excavations in Beaney Institute, High Street.

Chichester, Sussex
Roman walls by Orchard Street, Priory Park, Market Avenue, Westgate Fields. Original tribal capital, 'the Trundle' hill-fort and causeway camp, 3 miles (4.8 km) N, SU 877111.

Dover, Kent
Lighthouse in castle. Roman painted house, New Street.

Fishbourne, West Sussex
Wing of palace with mosaics, garden, sections of wall, bath suite, plans and models. Site museum. SU 841047, off A259 1½ miles (2.4 km) W of Chichester.

Holtye Common, Sussex
Section of Roman road, TQ 461391, off A264 5 miles (8 km) E of East Grinstead.

Lewes, Sussex
Lewes castle's Barbican Museum has collection of Romano-British relics from local sites.

Lullingstone, Kent
Villa with mosaics, Christian chapel, bath suite. TQ 530650, off A225 at Eynsford. (*See also final chapter.*)

Lympne, Kent
Scattered fort stones, TK 117342, visible from unclassified road off B2067 at Shepway Cross, E of Lympne village. (*See also final chapter.*)

Pevensey, East Sussex
Castle walls and bastions. (*See also final chapter.*)

Portchester, Hampshire
Castle walls, SU 625046. Exhibition dealing with Forts of the Saxon Shore. (*See also final chapter.*)

Reculver, Kent
Fragment of fort by ruins of Saxon church and Norman towers. (*See also final chapter.*)

Richborough, Kent
Fort walls and early earthworks. Base of triumphal arch. Site museum. (*See also first and final chapters.*)

Rockbourne, Hampshire
Villa foundations. Site museum. SU 120170, off B3078 3 miles (4.8 km) W of Fordingbridge.

Silchester, Hampshire
Perimeter walls, SU 640625, 1 mile (1.6 km) E of Silchester. Calleva museum on site, but major excavation displays in Reading Museum.

Vine leaves are interwoven with the hair of Autumn, in this mosaic of the Seasons at Cirencester.

SOUTH-WEST AND THE WESTERN MARCHES

IN one corner of the earthworks crowning Hod Hill in Dorset can be seen, during winter months when growth is sparse, outlines of Iron Age huts and storage pits packed into what was obviously a fair-sized community before the Romans came. Unlike some hill-forts this was not just a last refuge or a meeting-place for occasional religious ceremonials: it must have been in full-time occupation.

As news of the invasion spread across country, the bank and ditch were strengthened but failed to keep the attackers out. Once the fort had been overrun, the conquerors added further embankments in the far corner with gateways leading into a fort which was garrisoned for some years to watch over the undulating landscape. The whole thing is in an excellent state of preservation but not easy to view at close quarters as the property is in private hands.

Far mightier is Maiden Castle near Dorchester, an 'enormous many-limbed organism of an antediluvian time', as Thomas Hardy described it. During sectional excavations between 1934 and 1938 Dr (later Sir) Mortimer Wheeler confirmed the existence of several layers of occupation, beginning with a causewayed camp – that is, an enclosure with a number of entrances and intersecting trackways regularly used for gathering of stock and for pagan festivals – dating back to about 3000 BC. On top of this were laid Iron Age fortifications and then, in Julius Caesar's time, multiple ditches and ramparts. Tens of thousands of pebbles from Chesil Beach were piled up as ammunition for the leather slings of the defending Durotriges.

Vespasian's troops opened the assault on the sevenfold ramparts with a barrage from their more powerful catapults, the *ballistae*, which hurled fusillades of stones and iron bolts over the walls and against the eastern gateway. Under this covering fire the infantry pounded up the slope and smashed their way in. No quarter was shown. Men and women were hacked to pieces. One skeleton recovered by Wheeler's team had an iron arrowhead sunk in its spine; the skulls of others were hammered in, and one of them shows the penetration of a

A ballista, *or siege engine; this outsize crossbow could use metal bolts as well as stones.*

An iron dart from one of Vespasian's ballistae *lodged in the spine of a defender during the attack on Maiden Castle, Dorset.*

The quadruple ramparts of Maiden Castle follow the contours of a chalk hill set back from the main Downland ridge.

ballista bolt. In spite of the fury of the conflict it is clear that the defenders made time, or were allowed after the defeat, to bury their dead fittingly: much of the historical evidence comes from a cemetery in which mangled corpses were formally accompanied by the usual vessels of food and drink.

Late on in the Roman occupation a temple, still marked in the grass, was built within the abandoned fortress for reasons which have never been satisfactorily explained.

When the farther reaches of the west had been cleared up, two tribal towns were ordained for the *civitas* of the Durotriges – Durnovaria (Dorchester) and Lindinis (Ilchester) – though there are signs that until then some occupation of Maiden Castle was allowed to continue in a limited way. A road linked Dorchester with the old hill-fort and went on to the coast near Weymouth. Other highways struck west to Exeter and north-west to Ilchester.

It is worthy of note that in the agriculturally rich

The late Romano-Celtic temple within Maiden Castle, built with an inner shrine and surrounding ambulatory.

Tauros Trigaramus, symbolic bull, from Maiden Castle.

heartland of Wessex very few villas have been located. Over the whole swathe of Salisbury Plain and Cranborne Chase were numerous small settlements and primitive farms but no sign of any rich individual farmer. The likeliest explanation for this, and for a similar dearth in the Fens of eastern England, is that both regions were administered as imperial estates. Just as the emperor's representatives exercised monopoly control over industries such as lead and copper mining, and the navy had rights over Wealden iron, so certain agricultural areas were managed for the benefit of the legionary commissariat and worked by native tenants with little scope for personal profit or advancement.

Dorchester was built close to Maumbury Rings, a Stone Age henge sanctuary whose sacred circle was converted by its new neighbours into a small amphitheatre, squeezed today between the railway line and the road to Maiden Castle. Another relic, visible near Poundbury, is the trough of an earthen aqueduct which carried water 10 miles (16 km) from the river Frome along a winding, gently descending course into the town.

Central roundel of the pavement from Hinton St Mary, with a head believed to represent Christ, and the Chi-rho.

Within Dorchester there flourished during the third and fourth centuries a school of mosaicists whose style can be recognized in floors of villas throughout the region. The most impressive example is the great pavement from Hinton St Mary, now in the British Museum, showing a clash of beliefs between four pagan figures – though there have been attempts to identify them as four evangelists – and a head of Christ together with the *Chi-rho* symbol. This monogram, made up of the two initial letters of the Greek name for Christ, was adopted by the emperor Constantine when he accepted Christianity, and employed by other converts in mosaics, wall paintings, crockery, and pewter dishes. A less ambitious mosaic and hypocaust remain in Dorchester itself, in Colliton Park, and there is a fragment of wall in West Walks. The excellent museum in West High Street holds a huge cache of more than 20,000 coins and all the finds from Maiden Castle, together with diagrams and photographs telling its full story.

Ilchester, capital of the other branch of the Durotriges, has even less to show above ground than its sister town. But even as I write this chapter there is news of what could be one of the largest and least disturbed Romano-British cemeteries so far found in this country. Beside the Foss Way a mile or so outside the town, it came to light when land was being cleared for a housing estate, and is estimated to contain as many as 1500 graves, as well as two mysterious structures which have not yet been completely uncovered, but one of which may prove to be an early Christian church.

The westernmost of Rome's substantial settlements was at Isca Dumnoniorum (Exeter) in the *civitas* of the Dumnonii. Beyond it, no Roman road can be plotted with any assurance. Some must have existed for transport to and from the tin mines, though much of this is known to have been handled by sea. Cornish tin had been exported to the Continent long before the Romans coveted the trade for themselves. They used the tin largely in combination with lead to make pewter tableware. Some of the native miners probably had to accept imperial supervision, but otherwise seem to have continued much as before, living in settlements known as Rounds with no trace of Romanized street plans or rectilinear housing blocks. There were no towns and not a sign of a villa, with the possible exception of one freakishly angled building west of Camborne in a district of predominantly circular huts.

For centuries Exeter had little to exhibit of its Roman heritage until 1945, when the after-effects of German bombing necessitated clearance of devastated areas near the cathedral and shattered buildings within the city walls. An archaeological committee found that the Romano-British population had been densest in the lower parts of the city, where huts and timber houses lined the main road to the riverside quays. Roman tiles were found in Anglo-Saxon masonry of church ruins in South Street, and many shards of glass and pottery were recovered; but the material was so fragmented that little of it proved worthy of permanent display.

Mining was also carried on in the Mendips, mainly for lead and silver. Lumpy hillocks and pits around Charterhouse are testimony to the workings which were once so busy. As with other industries under direct imperial control, the authorities left their stamp on the product. Lead 'pigs' or ingots have been found as far away as France, bearing the impress of the Second Legion which had completed Vespasian's drive to the west. Dated ingots show that the mines were going strong under their new

managers within six years after the invasion. Near to Charterhouse are traces of houses of the period, and a small amphitheatre. Jacquetta Hawkes has engagingly suggested that the place must have had something of the atmosphere of a Wild West frontier town.

On the Severn bank north of the Mendips stood Abonae (Sea Mills), where foundations of a house with some wall and stone guttering remain from what was at first a patrol base for the Classis Britannica, and later a supply port connected by ferry with Venta Silurum (Caerwent) on the Welsh side of the river. Further east along that northern bank lies Lydney, from which a road drove straight to Ariconium (Weston-under-Penyard) through the Forest of Dean. Part of the road's paving, with its uncommon kerbstones, is maintained in the Forest to demonstrate the style of construction. The surroundings were another source of mineral wealth: iron was mined here for at least three centuries. There were also itinerant potters who used local clay and ochre in their wares and moved on when supplies of these and of timber for fuel had been exhausted.

Excavations between 1969 and 1976 at Corinium Dobunnorum (Cirencester) exposed a cemetery

This antefix from Dorchester must once have served as a gutter spout on a local building.

Solidi of Honorius and Arcadius, from Maiden Castle. They ruled jointly as emperors in the fifth century.

The Foss Way, photographed just west of Castle Cary, Somerset.

whose skeletons show that the commonest Romano-British ailment was arthritis, affecting almost half the adult population. One wonders if any of them sought relief in the not too distant spa of Aquae Sulis – waters of Sulis – which later came to be known simply as Bath. The curative powers of the warm mineral springs were not regarded merely as a natural phenomenon: the basin built around the source was dedicated to a combination of the Celtic goddess Sulis and the Roman goddess of healing, wisdom and the arts. Visitors threw coins, bracelets, brooches and other offerings into the waters as we might toss pennies into a wishing well. Many of these have been extracted from the drain and put on show. Among less agreeable contributions was a leaden curse tablet inscribed in reverse so that only the gods might decipher it, imploring that 'he who stole Vilbia from me may waste away as the waters' and proceeding to list Vinna and Verianus among a remarkable number of suspects – enough to suggest that the captivating Vilbia was a somewhat flighty and unreliable wench in the first place.

A leaden curse tablet found at Bath, calling down vengeance on 'he who stole Vilbia from me'.

The museum now enclosing the baths has a full-sized reconstruction of the façade of the Sulis-Minerva temple, bearing a Gorgon's head with serpentine hair and a raffish moustache. This once formed part of the shield of Minerva, whose bronze head is displayed near the cornerstones of an altar which stood before the shared temple. Coals from Somerset were burned during devotions at this altar. The swimming bath is still fed from its original stone culvert, and floored by lead which probably came from the Mendip mines. The Victorians misguidedly chose to add statues of emperors and anachronistic columns.

Use of lead in pipes, cisterns and baths must have seemed a good thing at the time, but some of its effects were not fully appreciated. As well as the symptoms of arthritis, rheumatism and gout among so many of the 450 skeletons of Cirencester, there were strikingly high concentrations of lead in most of the bones. Some children may even have died from lead poisoning because of the metal water pipes and cooking utensils.

The Great Bath of Aquae Sulis, now Bath, Avon.

This Medusa mask in Bath stone may represent a Gorgon's head, but some suggest it is a symbol of Sulis, the Celtic water deity linked here with Minerva.

In spite of their ailments and comparatively short lives – the average span for men was 40 years, for women around 38 – the citizens of Cirencester prospered from the riches of grain and wool sent to market from the extensive villas of the Cotswolds, until their city grew into the second largest in the province after London. Its present museum has also profited from those same villas and from the assets of the tribal capital itself in the shape of imported and native pottery, wall plaster, ornaments, and mosaic pavements featuring mythical creatures, the Seasons, and the popular theme of Orpheus charming animals with his lyre. Rewarding clues have been found in shop foundations around the wide forum: one shop seems to have been a butcher's, as bones and refuse were still detectable in pits below the floor.

An oil lamp found at Bath.

The East Bath, Bath.

A candle-holder from Bath, made in the shape of a stag.

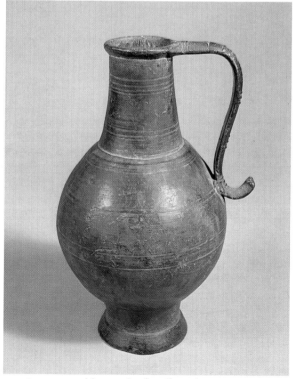

A bronze jug for oil or wine.

A local saying declares: 'Scratch Gloucestershire, find Rome.' It is true that the soil of the county covers – and occasionally disgorges – great treasures and luxuries of the past. Among the more lavish villas of the region are those at Witcombe, rediscovered in 1818, and Woodchester, whose Orphean floor is the most magnificent yet seen in England. It required about a million and a half cubes, laid by interior decorators from a Cirencester workshop who seem also to have been responsible for the mosaics of Chedworth not many miles away. Protection of the Woodchester masterpiece has meant that it must remain covered most of the time: it is opened to public view only once every ten years.

Chedworth villa is another of those whose reopening was the result of a lucky accident. Once again, someone was trying to dig out a ferret. Its wooded surroundings make it the most enviably placed of all gentlemen farmers' residences. Life in the well-appointed rooms with their central heating, tessellated floors and private courtyard must have

The Cirencester acrostic produced an apparently pagan invocation but concealed the letters of 'Pater Noster'.

Shorn of roofs and upper walls, a corner of Chedworth villa.

been very gracious and gratifying. The spring supplying water to the house has never run dry to this day. Yet in spite of the sylvan setting it did not remain purely a farmhouse: activities at one stage switched from agriculture to the manufacture of farm tools from Forest of Dean iron, and the use of Cotswold wool and fuller's earth in fulling – that is, cleansing and thickening cloth.

Villas of such elegance could not have been confidently built until the menace from the western frontier, too close for comfort, had been contained. Although Vespasian had effectively subdued the western fringes of the province in less than four years, the mountainous tracts of Wales proved more defiant. The defeated Caratacus continued to organize guerrilla raids back across the border. The Fourteenth and Twentieth Legions were stretched along a turbulent front between Gloucester and Chester, and for 30 years after the invasion made little progress against the Welsh tribes or their British immigrants who had sought alliances there.

Even after Caratacus had at last fallen into Roman hands there was little let-up. Claudius had envisaged the exploitation of the more easily governable lowlands and the establishment of a barrier of friendly or neutral tribes between Romanized England (if we can call it that, allowing for the fact that the name did not exist until bestowed by the Angles in a later age) and the wilder uplands to the west and north. He wanted no long-drawn-out war of attrition with unmanageable barbarians. His successors, however, found themselves afflicted by just that. Only in AD 74 did the governor Sextus Julius Frontinus throw everything into an all-out campaign which, starting in the southern fringes of Wales, struck inwards from the legionary fortress at Gloucester and, after seaborne assault from the Bristol Channel, from a fortress over the border at Isca (Caerleon). Between these two military emplacements grew up the capital of a *civitas* for the subdued Silures at Venta Silurum (Caerwent).

In spite of its importance as a veterans' *colonia*

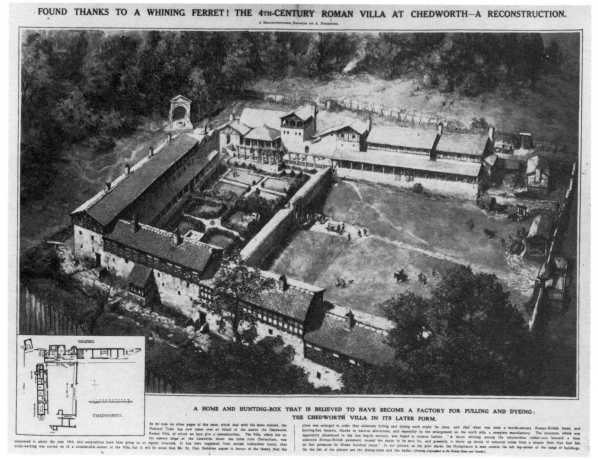

FOUND THANKS TO A WHINING FERRET! THE 4TH-CENTURY ROMAN VILLA AT CHEDWORTH—A RECONSTRUCTION.
A Reconstruction Drawing by A. Forestier.

A HOME AND HUNTING-BOX THAT IS BELIEVED TO HAVE BECOME A FACTORY FOR FULLING AND DYEING: THE CHEDWORTH VILLA IN ITS LATER FORM.

Chedworth villa as it had developed by the fourth century, with fulling and dyeing workshops in the northern range.

A reconstruction drawing of Wroxeter in its days as a major provincial city, when it covered 170 acres (85 ha).

Gloucester tombstone of Rufus Sita, a 1st-century Thracian cavalryman who died at 40 after 22 years' service

and protector of the southern end of the Welsh marches, Gloucester has forgotten most of its legionary foundation. Roads from Cirencester and from the Forest of Dean iron-workings carry few ghosts. Even the medieval overlay of the city has been hideously maltreated by modern planning vandals. If we want to hear whispers of the men who marched to defend this frontier we need to seek out the string of border forts through Leintwardine in Herefordshire and Titterstone Clee in Shropshire to that early auxiliary outpost at Chester which was enlarged into a full-scale legionary fortress. The supply route of Watling Street was extended to meet this road at Cornoviorum Viroconium (Wroxeter).

> Today the Roman and his trouble
> Are ashes under Uricon.

So wrote A.E. Housman about Viroconium (or Uriconium) in *A Shropshire Lad*. Wroxeter is in fact less ashen and somehow more evocative than Gloucester. It became the centre of a *civitas* only after serving as a station in the defence chain and after the legionary headquarters had been moved to Chester. The troops' departure caused no damage to the town's finances: it grew into the fourth largest in the province. Dedicated to the emperor Hadrian, the town forum can still be located, and there are remains of the basilican town hall's colonnade. The ramparts are overgrown but solid enough, and there is a section of the public baths wall and its accom-

The 'Old Work' at Wroxeter, remains of a wall that separated the exercise hall and the baths in the foreground.

Archaeological excavation in progress at Wroxeter.

panying exercise area – unusually, there was a swimming bath here although Wroxeter had no pretensions to being a spa. The church has quite an amalgam of Roman, Saxon and Norman materials.

North from Wroxeter to Whitchurch the road is generally classified as Watling Street West, joining another branch road from Penkridge in Staffordshire and pressing on until it crosses the river Dee into the city of Chester.

Deva (Chester) was the home of the Twentieth Legion for the larger part of the Roman occupation, and in Chester's Grosvenor Museum an exhibition has been built round the life of the military. It contains weapons and monuments, personal belongings of the soldiers and their womenfolk, and one loving tombstone dedicated to Cocceia Irene, the sorrowing widower's 'most chaste and pure wife'. The unusual construction of the celebrated

Roman mirrors were usually made of speculum, but this decorated mirror from Wroxeter is of silver.

Tombstone of Caecilius, an optio – *a non-commissioned officer serving under a centurion – at Chester.*

An altar dedicated to 'The Genius of the Century' at Chester.

Columns in the amphitheatre at Chester.

medieval Rows with their first-floor shopping galleries may have been dictated by the dimensions of the well-nigh indestructible Roman foundations along the streets. Rather than attempt the demolition of these heavy stone courses it was found more practical to set tiered frontages upon them and enclose the first-floor walkways under oversailing upper storeys.

The city walls, too, rest on Roman foundations. Much of the northern section has been preserved at its original parapet level. By the Roman Gardens is an amphitheatre, and by the Wolf Gate an angle tower. Remains of the city quays stand beside the ancient course of the river Dee, between the wall and the racecourse.

Containment of the Welsh and concentration of

military power against the northern uplands allowed the growth of confidence and civil amenities across central England. Left to run their own affairs, the *civitates* raised money to develop and beautify their towns, encouraging local markets and local craftsmen. Smiths, shoemakers and carpenters ceased to be itinerant traders or part-time odd job men and came in from the villages to seek urban premises with a guaranteed turnover. Wine merchants tempted the newly discerning palates of the British. Comfort was proving more agreeable than tribal pride.

PLACES TO VISIT

Bath, Avon
Roman Baths Museum incorporating Great Bath and reconstruction of temple frontage.

Charterhouse, Somerset
Remains of amphitheatre from lead-mining settlement. ST 501561, unclassified road off B3135/3371 5 miles (8 km) E of Cheddar.

Chedworth, Gloucestershire
Villa with mosaics, bath suite, servants' quarters. SP 053135, *National Trust*, in Chedworth Woods off A429 (the Foss Way) 7 miles (11.2 km) NE of Cirencester.

Chester, Cheshire
City walls. Roman Army gallery in Grosvenor Museum.

Cirencester, Gloucestershire
Amphitheatre, Cotswold Avenue. Corinium Museum, Park Street, with mosaics, sculpture, domestic items, and reconstructions of a mosaicist's workshop and of a villa dining-room and kitchen.

Dorchester, Dorset
Town house in Colliton Park. Maumbury Rings amphitheatre beside A354 S of town. Country Museum displays material from local excavations including Hod Hill and Maiden Castle, and an Iron Age anchor found not far from Poole Harbour.

Forest of Dean, Gloucestershire
Short preserved stretch of Roman road, off B4431 2 miles (3.2 km) NW of Blakeney.

Kings Weston, Avon
Villa with mosaics and wall sections. ST 534775, off B4057 4 miles (6.4 km) NW of Bristol.

Ludlow, Shropshire
Ludlow Museum, Butter Cross, has Roman exhibits.

Maiden Castle, Dorset
Hill-fort with foundations of late Romano-British temple. SY 669884, off A354 2 miles (3.2 km) SW of Dorchester.

Poundbury, Dorchester, Dorset
Early Iron Age fort and embankment of Romano-British aqueduct.

Sea Mills, near Avonmouth, Avon
Foundations of Roman house and fragments of *Abonae* port walls. ST 556 758.

Titterstone Clee Hill, Shropshire
Border fort, SO 592779, above unclassified roads between A4117 and B4364 6 miles (9.6 km) E of Ludlow.

Witcombe, Great Witcombe, Gloucestershire
Villa with mosaics and hypocaust. SO 899142, *Dept of the Environment*, off A436 5 miles (8 km) SE of Gloucester.

Wotton-under-Edge, Gloucestershire
Modern replica of the buried Woodchester pavement, made by local mosaicists and displayed at the Rev. Rowland Hill's Tabernacle Church over Easter and Spring Bank Holiday weekends, and from 1 June to 30 September, except for Mondays other than Bank Holidays.

Wroxeter, Shropshire
Public baths and colonnade. Site museum. Other finds in Shrewsbury Museum. ST 565087, on B4380 5 miles (8 km) SE of Shrewsbury.

A statuette of the emperor Nero accoutred as Alexander the Great, found near Needham Market in Suffolk.

THE MIDLANDS AND EASTERN ENGLAND

SOUTH of Coventry stands the replica of a strongpoint which may once have contributed to the suppression of Boudicca's rebellion. The Lunt Fort at Baginton was set up in the year of that revolt, with a deep ditch and wide ramparts bearing a wooden palisade and a parapet for the defenders. It was probably erected on the orders of Suetonius Paulinus as a mustering camp for legionaries summoned from Anglesey and other positions to counter the Icenian threat. The final battle against the warrior queen was considered such a triumph that the accolade of *Martia Victrix* was bestowed on the Fourteenth Legion, and it could have been at the same time that the title *Victrix* was granted to the Twentieth Legion. Speculation about the scene of that confrontation has usually centred on the Midlands, not far from the Lunt.

In recent years a reconstruction of the fort has been supervised by the Herbert Museum, Coventry, using only tools and techniques which would have been available to its original builders. A recreation of the timbered eastern gateway stands between turf and timber ramparts 25 ft (8 m) high; and further restoration is promised for the future.

Another echo of the turbulent Iceni can be found further east, near Cherry Hinton on the outskirts of Cambridge. Here the fieldworks known as the War Ditches date from that crucial time when the Romans insisted on disarming various tribes, thereby sowing the seeds of resentment which were to germinate into bloody conflict.

When the harsh measures of the victors had been toned down and it had been agreed to restore some measure of self-government to the Iceni, a *civitas*

Modern reconstruction of the gateway and defences, with a palisaded parapet, of the Lunt Fort.

Crop marks within the ramparts of Caistor St Edmund, Norfolk, show up the street plan of the Icenian capital after the tribe's post-Boudiccan resettlement.

was delineated for them with its capital at Venta Icenorum (Caistor St Edmund) in Norfolk. The inhabitants do not seem to have taken readily to Romanized ways of living. Although their township had the usual formal plan, still recognizable in crop marks viewed from the air, with dark lines which may have been gutters running down the middle of the streets, they continued to make use of their native huts until well into the next century. Then more civilized houses came into being, together with a forum, basilica, and public baths. In due course thick walls and four gateways were added, with a ditch round the outside.

The area enclosed was small and never increased to any appreciable size. No later Norman or medieval town sprang from it: the foremost city of the region, Norwich, was a separate entity of which there is no trace before the tenth century. Unlike that later settlement, Venta Icenorum was served

The four survivors of the Bartlow Hills near Ashdon in Essex, first-century tumuli in which rich grave-goods were found eighteen centuries later.

A stretch of the Peddar's Way near Fring in Norfolk. This prehistoric trackway from the North Norfolk coast into Breckland was taken over by the Romans, and in 1907 a hoard of Romano-British coins was found beside it, together with skulls and a skeleton, an iron spear, and copious shards of pottery.

not by a readily navigable river but only by the stream of the Tas. Its trade is thought to have been deviously channelled through a small port 20 miles (32 km) away at what is now Caister-on-Sea. In its first rough-and-ready form this had a low bank and stockade to which thick flint walls were later added. Among its remains are foundations of what appears to have been a hostel for seamen loading and unloading, waiting for a shipment or a tide; and part of the wall and gateway can still be seen.

Evidence of villas is scanty in Norfolk and Suffolk. Even the route of the Icknield Way, beside which one might have expected the usual crop of prosperous farmsteads, has yielded little more than fragments of the most rudimentary style of cottage. There are grounds for supposing that the Iceni, even when resettled, were not allowed the same opportunities for personal advancement as other tribesmen, and that tracts of the countryside were operated as imperial estates – as were the neighbouring Fens – under direct Roman control. The green track of Old Hundred Lane, crossing the Roman road which has become the A140 near Waltham

Hall, could well be the boundary of such an estate, with a not too highly placed official housed in the plain little villa found at Stonham Aspal.

Villages and hamlets accommodated most of the labour force. One example was discovered in 1961 to the west of the long, broad street of Long Melford in Suffolk, where a Belgic settlement had been re-organized in Roman fashion and occupied until at least the fourth century. More was exposed in 1970 when clearance for a housing estate brought to light a length of Roman road surfaced with compacted sand and flint, and other layers of lime and pebbles. It was on the direct line of that road known to have linked the Trinovantes' capital of Caesaromagus (Chelmsford) with the Peddar's Way to and from the Wash. Neighbouring finds included bronze pins and a variety of brooches, one of them in the style associated with Colchester workshops before Boudicca razed them to the ground. There was also an infant burial, apparently of a stillborn baby.

More impressive burials were made on the border of Essex and Cambridgeshire. A couple of miles north of Ashdon stand the Bartlow Hills, four

The burial mound on Mersea Island, Essex.

A glass bowl containing cremation ashes, found in a leaden casket within a tiled chamber, inside the Mersea burial mound.

survivors of eight huge mounds which were tunnel-
led into between 1832 and 1840 to reveal cremated
remains and grave goods. The mounds are so
majestic and their contents so numerous that ro-
mantics have inevitably suggested that Boudicca
herself was interred here. Certainly the occupants of
the chambers were accompanied by impressive
offerings of food and wine within bronze, glass and
pottery vessels. There were bowls of Samian ware,
jugs and perfume bottles, ornaments, and bathers'
strigils. Unfortunately the hoard was taken home by
Lord Maynard to Easton Lodge, and destroyed in
the fire which gutted the building in 1847.

On the island of Mersea, which legionary engineers linked to the mainland by a causeway, a truly
Roman mausoleum was found with spokes thrust-
ing out to make a wheel tomb similar to those
outside the Eternal City itself. Not far from the
scene of this discovery stands a mound about 20 ft
(6 m) high, a good 100 ft (31 m) in circumference,
which housed just one glass bowl of cremation
ashes, set within a casket which in its turn was
enclosed in a small chamber lined with tiles. These
sparse contents of the mount are now in Colchester
castle. And one other Mersea feature is recalled just

*Pieces of a bronze ceremonial mace from
Willingham Fen.*

Bronze figurines from Willingham Fen: they were probably votive offerings.

by a name: Pharos Lane, the only surviving record of the existence of a lighthouse whose base has now been obscured by modern building.

Obviously the Romans found it worth their while to exploit the creeks and inlets of coast and estuary, in Essex as elsewhere. They were also expert in disciplining inland waterways. After the armies had moved north, fording the Ouse at Godmanchester and setting up a fort there to control the crossing – savaged by Boudicca but renewed and transformed into a residential and agricultural centre – assessments were made of supply routes to the far-stretched forces. Rivers and artificial canals could be just as effective as roads for many goods, and in the Fenlands it cost less to convert and divert these than to import stone metalling into a boggy area with little building material of its own to offer.

During the Iron Age there had been few settlements in the region because of repeated flooding. By a lucky chance for the invaders, soon after their

The Norman arches of Ickleton church in Cambridgeshire are supported on pillars brought from Roman buildings here or in neighbouring Great Chesterford.

arrival there occurred a slight but valuable lowering of water levels. They were able to cut new channels and navigable cuts with towpaths, and to some extent control the flow of the waters. No private farmers or speculators built their luxury villas here. The prevalence of small hamlets suggests that groups of smallholders could have been granted short-term concessions from the imperial supervisors of drainage, production of grain, meat, salt and leather, transport to the legions on the borders, and exports to Continental garrisons or markets. Only on the periphery do we find the occasional individual dwelling such as the villa and its basilican companion at Ickleton in Cambridgeshire – and that was most probably the residence of a senior official, conceivably working in liaison with the garrison of the 30-acre (12-ha) military camp across the river Granta, or Cam, at Great Chesterford.

Cambridge itself was of no great importance during this era. A palisaded enclosure set up soon after the conquest was replaced by a simple fort of whose interior buildings there is now no trace. In the second century a larger enclosure was supplied with streets and houses, but did not flourish: although a handful of people continued to live there, many buildings were left derelict. The only known employment for the inhabitants was digging out marl and gravel. After the Romans had gone the whole site was abandoned.

One of the navigation engineers' most valuable legacies was the Car Dyke, possibly hewn out under military supervision by the cowed Iceni. Its two main sections effectively connected the productions of the region with Lincoln and York. The southern cut, fragmented now and little more than a congested ditch, was a barge route and drainage channel from the river Cam at Waterbeach, through the earthworks of what must have been quite a busy community at Cottenham, to the Great Ouse near Aldreth. The northern section left the river Nene close to Water Newton for its destination at the *colonia* of Lincoln, from which the Foss Dyke later added an extension to the Trent. Along its way the Car Dyke collected water from the shallow slopes for discharge into the Nene and Witham. It supplied food to the northern garrisons, and to a lesser extent served as a distribution route for finished goods from the Nene potteries. Like Josiah Wedgwood in a later age, the potters realized that breakages would be fewer during the smooth progress of a water-borne barge than on the bumpy, jarring roads.

POTTERY

The most fashionable pottery throughout the Empire was Samian ware, so called because of its resemblance to a glossy red ceramic style supposedly originating from the Aegean island of Samos. Decorated with floral or animal figures, it imitated silversmiths' relief work by packing the clay into prepared moulds. Large quantities were imported into Britain from factories in Gaul. In the second century attempts were made to establish an indigenous industry at Colchester and much later at Oxford and York, without much success.

For everyday use the Romano-British made do with coarse unglazed pots, bowls, lamps, tankards and kitchen mortars. Many were crudely made at home, but gradually a number of regional workshops began to offer more consistent results from accurately controlled kilns. Small-scale industrial

A third-century beaker from Castor or nearby in the Nene valley, inspired by Rhenish models.

A hemispherical bowl of Samian ware, with an echinus *or moulding separating the rim from the ornamented lower section.*

villages grew up in the New Forest, in Cambridgeshire around Cherry Hinton and Horningsea, and around several sites in Norfolk. Manduessedum (Mancetter) in Warwickshire beside Watling Street was a distribution centre for a complex of factories in its immediate vicinity. Gloucester produced what archaeologists distinguish as 'Glevum ware', though the actual premises have never been discovered; near Farnham in Surrey a distinctive grey and white product became the most popular for miles around.

Of all indigenous products the more ambitious Castor ware was the most highly regarded. Grey or slightly coppery in hue, it imitated Samian ware to some extent in its animal figures, especially in hunting scenes; but the designs were piped on, as with a wedding cake, instead of being moulded. Manufacture flourished along the Nene Valley, and trim little housing estates sprang up for well-to-do managers. At Castor in Cambridgeshire there was a central guild or trade hall, with warehouses around a large courtyard, complete with a bath block – like pit showers today? – and a shrine which could have been that of some patron deity of potters. Quays beside the river served a steady barge traffic.

A first-century rusticated jar from Colchester.

A dark-coated Castor-ware beaker from Colchester dating from the second or third century, with a chariot race relief in a kaolin paste known as barbotine.

A Terra Rubra flask from Colchester, dating from the first century.

New Forest potteries in the third and fourth centuries made hard ware with a lustrous surface, sometimes, as here, painted with white ornamentation.

A whole string of forts, no two more than a day's march apart, marked the northern thrust of the legions. Immediately to the east of Castor was Longthorpe marching camp, expanded during the trouble with the Iceni but abandoned when the Ninth Legion was officially concentrated on Lincoln. Across the river, another fort was not so brusquely discarded. Where Ermine Street, the A1, the Nene Valley Railway and the river run in brief proximity west of Peterborough (under whose cathedral were once other potteries) there thrusts up the bulky earthwork of Durobrivae (Water Newton). Its first clay bank defences were duly reinforced by a stone wall and, in the fourth century, stone bastions. A special barrier to the east guarded against flood waters over the marshy levels. Quite apart from its industrial suburb at Castor, Water Newton itself was as much a commercial centre as a military or residential one: most of its identifiable buildings have proved to be of the standard house-cum-shop construction, and one of the largest must have been a market hall or senate house, or both combined.

The extent of the town's development is mirrored in a hoard of silver found buried there, perhaps to hide it from religious persecutors. The equivalent of a set of church plate, it is the earliest collection of objects marked with Christian symbols yet found in the Roman world. A large dish with the *Chi-rho* monogram had been loaded with a silver goblet, an intricately chased flagon, a number of votive plaques of which several also bore the monogram, and a golden disc on which those letters were accompanied by a symbol of Alpha and Omega, the Beginning and the End. Since the community survived long after the emperor Domitian's harassment of Christians had given way to official approval of their beliefs, one wonders why it was never dug

Silver cup with pedestal and handles, from Water Newton.

Also from Water Newton, three silver plaques with Chi-rho *monograms.*

A silver jug decorated with scrolls and leaves from Water Newton.

up again by the owners' descendants; unless, of course, it was buried or reburied much later when Saxon raids grew more frequent.

From the Nene valley three thoroughfares headed for Lincoln: Ermine Street, King Street, and the Car Dyke. Not many miles up Ermine Street the outlines of another fort were recorded by aerial photography in 1959. Here at Great Casterton an extensive town had developed by the late second century, and soon after that some influential citizen built himself a large aisled barn about a quarter of a mile from the original fort, perhaps for a bailiff and staff to run his farming enterprise on his behalf. It was equipped with a corn-drying floor which is thought to have had a conical roof, much in the style of a Kentish oast-house and with much the same purpose. After a fire late in the fourth century it was not restored, but a corn-drying oven was set up in the ruins.

Ermine Street cuts across a corner of the adjacent territories of the quelled Iceni and the less aggressive Coritani. A few fortlets hereabouts may have been installed to keep the two apart and frustrate any concerted rebellion. The *civitas* of the more amenable tribe had its centre at Ratae Coritanorum (Leicester): indeed, it was graciously allowed to retain its cantonal capital on the site of its original settlement. Some of the Romano-British floors now lie beneath the railway station and a shop near St Nicholas's church, but above ground near that church is an impressive stone wall known for some remote reason as the Jewry Wall. It overlooks what was once the exercise hall of the public baths, whose foundations are still clearly marked. In the suburb of Aylestone the Raw Dykes were part of an aqueduct which supplied the baths with water.

Another link in the chain of fortifications along Ermine Street was at Causennae (Ancaster), watching over a gap through which the river Witham flowed in ancient times. It had to be refurbished and brought back into commission during the confusions of the fourth century, as indicated in finds of coins from that period.

Coins, like pottery, offer invaluable aid in the dating of settlements and events. Their widespread use was one of the benefits bestowed by Rome on the everyday dealings of its subject races and deferential allies. Even when primitive tribes had improved their agricultural and manufacturing skills, and learned to construct tolerably sound huts in place of caves and hovels, their mutual commerce often remained clumsy and laborious. For a considerable time the common tokens of exchange were iron bars, which may have been an improvement on the

This relief shows tribesmen attacking a Roman fort with a battering ram and archers.

complications of bartering cattle against cloth, and grain against spearheads, but still left a lot to be desired in accurate calculation and the issue of small change. Increasing use of portable coinage has come to be regarded as a yardstick of a people's development.

Coins introduced by Belgic settlers from Europe became acceptable currency, and the dispersion of various incoming tribes throughout the country can be plotted from the distribution of coins carelessly dropped in forts and villages, hoarded under living quarters, or buried in time of war. Imitative British chieftains began minting their own money. Commius and his son Tincommius of the Atrebates used the tribal emblem of a triple-tailed horse, and Tincommius sedulously employed Roman die-cutters. Tasciovanus, king of the Catuvellauni in about 20 BC, issued coins from St Albans and Colchester, and his mightier son Cunobelinus followed suit with the emblem of an ear of corn. Later Verica of the Atrebates, perhaps to display his pro-Roman leanings, employed the motif of a vine-leaf.

There was no guarantee that such regional tokens would be freely negotiable between one tribe and another, especially during times of friction. Rome imposed an international currency and utilized it for propaganda as well as purely monetary purposes. When Claudius had achieved his ambition of annexing Britain he introduced a proud personal note by displaying his head on one side of a coin and a triumphal arch with the name of Britannia on the reverse. Later mintings continued the promotion of the imperial cult as well as providing a uniform means of exchange. Along with this was introduced a standard system of weights and measures.

It is sadly true that coins were easier to mislay than iron bars, by dropping them or having them stolen. At Bath we came across a curse tablet lamenting the theft of a woman. Another leaden tablet was found south-west of Nottingham that recorded a theft of money from one Canius Dignus and implored Jupiter to wreak vengeance via the thief's memory, intestines, heart, marrow and veins. The supplicant offered a tithe of the sum if the god could recover his money. Disappointingly we have no record of whether Jupiter did intervene or, if so, whether he received his promised percentage.

All roads lead, it was once boasted, to Rome. A glance at the map suggests that in north-eastern England in those days most roads headed towards Lindum (Lincoln).

Inside the Newport Arch, the third-century north gate of the Lincoln colonia.

The town was founded as a base for the Ninth Legion, known as the Hispana because of its Spanish connections. An early minor fort for auxiliaries may have preceded it, but a more substantial one was erected shortly after AD 50, consisting of a ditch and an earth and timber rampart shielding an area within which the later cathedral and castle were to rise. When after some 20 to 30 years it was designated a *colonia* for legionary veterans they were given homes and land within and without a new wall and a wider ditch. Many houses were in the affluent bracket, and the whole *colonia* was well catered for and cleansed. Under all the main streets were stone-built sewers with smaller drains along the way and manholes at regular intervals.

Stretches of wall survive behind a hotel car park and one or two private gardens. The ditch can be seen in Temple Gardens and the garden of the local art gallery. Excavations in 1959 and 1960 disinterred the foundations of the eastern gateway, one tower of which has been kept in front of the Eastgate Hotel. More visually remarkable is the Newport Gate, once the northern entrance to the town. Modern traffic passes through its central arch, and one of the two pedestrian arches to either side is still in use. The apparent squatness of the main arch is misleading: when it was built, the road level was 8 ft (2.4 m) lower than at present.

From this gateway Ermine Street strode off towards the Humber. From the ferry terminal at Petuaria (Brough) on the north bank, roads went to Derventio (Malton) in North Yorkshire and its auxiliary group fort, or to the new headquarters into which the Ninth Legion marched from Lincoln – a base destined to be, in Roman times and long after, the key fortress of the north.

PLACES TO VISIT

Baginton, near Coventry, Warwickshire
Replica of the Lunt Fort, SP 345752, off A45 S of Coventry.

Bartlow Hills, near Ashdon, Essex
Romano-British burial mounds on Cambridgeshire border. TL 587448, beside unclassified road 2 miles (3.2 km) N of Ashdon.

Bradwell-on-Sea, Essex
Wall fragment of Fort of the Saxon Shore near early Saxon church and nuclear power station. TM 031082, reached by Roman track, 2 miles (3.2 km) E of B1021. (*See also final chapter.*)

Burgh Castle, Norfolk
Walls and bastions of Fort of the Saxon Shore. TG 475046, 3 miles (4.8 km) W of Great Yarmouth on minor road from junction of A12 and A143. (*See also final chapter.*)

Caister-on-Sea, Norfolk
Remains of wall, gateway and inner buildings. TG 518125, between A149 and A1064 on NW outskirts.

Caistor St Edmund, Norfolk
Earthworks of Venta Icenorum accessible only by causeway across ditch to rampart near church. TG 230035, minor road off A140 4 miles (6.4 km) S of Norwich.

Car Dyke
Several sections visible in Cambridgeshire and Lincolnshire, notably between Landbeach and Cottenham, Cambridgeshire, and from near Water Newton, Cambridgeshire, northwards to Lincoln. TL 476688; TL 483671; TF 063690.

Cherry Hinton, Cambridgeshire
Earthworks of the War Dykes on the outskirts of Cambridge, between Cherry Hinton village and Cambridge Airport.

Cockley Cley, Norfolk
Conjectural reconstruction of Iceni village from time of Boudicca. TF 793042, minor road off A1065 3 miles (4.8 km) SW of Swaffham.

Colchester, Essex
(*See page 45 for details.*)

Gog Magog Hills, Cambridgeshire
A Roman road can be walked several miles to site of Roman settlement at Horseheath. TL 546493, off A604 3 miles (4.8 km) SE of Cambridge, or at Horseheath, TL 615476.

Leicester, Leicestershire
Bath foundations and Jewry Wall, St Nicholas Street. Raw Dykes beside southbound A526 at suburb of Aylestone.

Lincoln, Lincolnshire
Newport Arch, Bailgate. East Gate foundations. Fragments of wall and south-west gate.

The tombstone of Valerius, a standard-bearer of the Ninth Legion at Lincoln.

Mersea Island, Essex
Cremation tumulus with access to burial chamber. TM 022143, off B1025 at island end of Roman causeway.

Peddar's Way, Norfolk
Prehistoric track improved by Romans from Holme-next-the-Sea through Castle Acre and Thetford into Suffolk. Many stretches good for walking. A well-marked section can be picked up at TF 844094 near A47 roundabout 2 miles (3.2 km) E of Swaffham.

Wall, Staffordshire
Remains of bath-house and posting station. Site museum. SK 098066, off A5 2 miles (3.2 km) SW of Lichfield.

Water Newton, Cambridgeshire
Earthworks of *Durobrivae* beside A1.

A section of 'Wade's Causeway'. Over a mile survives on Wheeldale Moor, North Yorkshire.

YORK AND THE NORTH

EBORACUM (York) became the new depot of the Ninth Legion when Vespasian, who had himself served in the conquest of Britain and by AD 69 was emperor, found it necessary to step up action against widespread revolts by the Brigantes. Here was to be the nerve centre of operations for holding down the northern reaches of the province and for pressing on against the Caledonians over the border. Here, too, at another time of stress came Hadrian to deal with the troubles of that border. When the country was divided by Septimius Severus at the end of the second century into two administrative sections, with London as capital of Britannia Superior, York became capital of Britan-

A section of York's medieval wall above the brick and stone courses of the Roman wall.

Interior of York's Multangular Tower, the western corner of the legionary base's defences.

Brick ducting for the hypocaust of extensive baths at Roman ground level, on view under the Roman Bath Inn.

nia Inferior. Severus died here. So did Constantius Chlorus while mounting an expedition against the Picts and Scots; and here his son Constantine's troops insisted on proclaiming the young man as emperor of Western Rome at a time when authority in the Empire itself had also been divided.

Constantine had for some time been held as a virtual hostage by the emperor Diocletian, who was suspicious of the possible ambitions of his deputy Caesar, Constantius. During that uneasy period he witnessed Diocletian's misguided attempts to revive the old Roman religion and outlaw the growing faith in Christianity. Mementoes of those and other days of persecution come to light in unexpected places. Among a number of smithies unearthed in Manchester in 1982 was found a fragment of wine jar with an inscription like that of the celebrated acrostic in Cirencester museum. Although on the face of it the cryptogram seems to praise Arepo, the sower who 'guides wheels with care', rearrangement of the letters produces 'Paternoster' twice, laid out as a cross with the A and O of Alpha and Omega at each tip. It is believed that this word-play became a secret code among Christians covertly acknowledging one another. Use was also made of the *Chi-rho*

Inside a Roman sewer in York.

monogram, but not openly until after Constantine's own conversion.

Preparing to fight a rival contender for the imperial purple, Constantine claimed to have been vouchsafed a vision of a cross in the sky, with the Greek words for 'in this, conquer'. He at once had the *Chi-rho* device painted on his soldiers' shields; and, after defeating his opponent, adopted Christianity and made it the official religion of the state, including Britain. A Christian bishop was installed at York, but the see did not survive the pagan onslaught of the Saxons.

York Minster today stands on the site of Roman military headquarters and retains some of its masonry, including the pillar facing the south door. Stonegate and Petergate were the two main streets, intersecting at the centre of the fortress and leading to gates in the walls. Large remnants of wall, with medieval additions, are still solidly in place, most obviously near the Multangular Tower forming the western corner of the fortress, and the eastern tower by Merchant Taylors' Hall. The Roman Bath Inn displays to its customers a glassed-over corner of the baths and hypocaust which once continued across most of the square outside; and in the cellar of the Treasurer's House are a slice of Roman street and the base of a pillar.

The town remained more markedly Roman than most in its time, though its shops and craftsmen were largely British, fashioning and selling ornaments of copper, bronze, and Whitby jet, many for export to the Continent. A few immigrant dealers seem to have been connected with the wine trade and other import and export businesses. In due course the settlement of retired soldiers from many countries which grew up outside the military establishment was given the honorary status of *colonia*. York was never adapted as the tribal centre of a *civitas*: when defeated and split up, the dominant Brigantes of the region were given quite another site.

According to the Egyptian geographer Ptolemy, the Brigantian confederation held sway across northern England 'from sea to sea'. There are conflicting opinions about the composition of this league of clans, and conflicting evidence from coins; but it would seem that a predominantly Celtic aristocracy had imposed itself upon earlier settlers and sought to unite them into a miniature nation. Their *oppidum* was probably the hill-fort of Almondbury, near Huddersfield.

A domestic group : Julia Velva's family on her tombstone in York.

In the early years of the takeover the Brigantes had collaborated with Rome. The colonizers were glad to have a buffer state of such dimensions between them and the wilder tribes of the far north. When Caratacus, after seven years of sporadic raiding from within Wales, was at last defeated in a major battle and made his way into the Pennines to seek an alliance with Cartimandua, queen of the Brigantes, he found that her alliance was still with the Empire: she handed him over in chains. In spite of the trouble the warrior chieftain had caused, Claudius behaved with unusual clemency. After parading Caratacus with his wife, family and vassals triumphantly through Rome, the emperor was so impressed by his pride of bearing and courageous speech that he allowed him to live on in honourable retirement.

It may have been as a direct consequence of Cartimandua's rejection of Caratacus that a split appeared in the kingdom. Her husband Venutius and a number of his men were dismayed by this betrayal of a heroic resistance fighter, and longed to take up his mantle. After a bitter quarrel Venutius led his followers northwards and built a huge embanked fort at Stanwick, near Scotch Corner. His deserted queen arrested a number of his relatives and proclaimed his ex-squire her new royal consort.

Once Venutius had enlisted enough support for his cause and calculated that Roman intervention was unlikely because of confusion in Rome itself after the death of Nero, he decided to return and overthrow Cartimandua. His attack was so vigorous that she had to send an urgent appeal for Roman support. A detachment of auxiliaries succeeded in halting Venutius and driving him back to Stanwick, where he added further fortifications and set about recruiting more allies.

Established as emperor after the squabbles in Rome were over, Vespasian turned his attention to his old battlegrounds and realized the danger of allowing Venutius time to build up reserves. He sent in a new governor, Petillius Cerialis, who had commanded the Ninth Legion against Boudicca and been routed by her. More experienced now, he risked no repetition of earlier misjudgments. Forts were established at Brough and Malton, and his old legion took possession of the fortress specially built at York.

The Ninth marched upon Stanwick while a pincer movement was made from the west under its

A statue of Mars, god of war, found in York.

legate, Gnaeus Julius Agricola. After a ferocious last stand, the subdued remnants of the Brigantes were allowed back into imperial favour only after certain sacrifices had been conceded. A much contracted *civitas* replaced the extensive kingdom, with its capital at Isurium Brigantium (Aldborough). A large part of the original territory was kept under military government, and some of it was handed over to the *colonia* at Lincoln and later that at York.

Large-scale warfare with the Brigantes had ended, but there were still elements bent on continuing guerrilla tactics from bleak hideouts in the Pennines. To counter these the military built forts and linking roads. One sympathizes with troops from warmer climes who found themselves on duty in the lonely wastes around Rey Cross and Greta Bridge. Under those same slopes, soldiers not

The remains of the south-western corner of town wall which enclosed the 60 acres (30 ha) of Aldborough, civitas *capital of the Brigantes.*

At Vinovia (Binchester, near Bishop Auckland), a cavalry fort had two rooms heated by hypocausts, one with a floor still supported by brick piers stamped with the mark of army artificers.

A bronze and silvered parade helmet for ceremonial occasions from Ribchester. Its crown carries embossed battle scenes, and there are relief figures on the thin visor-mask.

The remains of the granaries at Ribchester cavalry fort in Lancashire. Ribchester fort was a local administrative centre and also incorporated a small settlement of Sarmatian veterans, natives of what is now southern Russia.

enjoying their training at modern Catterick may derive some slight comfort from the thought that they are not the first: the Cataractonium legionary fortress was in operation centuries ago.

A fort that served from early times until the end of the Roman occupation, with only one short gap, stands above Bainbridge in Wensleydale. In its earliest form it had an earth rampart and some timber buildings, but after AD 160 there were reinforcements in stone. The garrison was no mere token force: it had to contend with a number of tribal assaults, and needed considerable rebuilding after being overrun towards the end of the second century, when extra barracks for an auxiliary unit were added.

Julius Agricola, who had played his part in the defeat of the Brigantes at Stanwick, was to see more of the province. After service in Rome and Aquitania he was appointed governor of Britain. His first task was to tackle the Ordovices in North Wales, who just before his arrival had annihilated an auxiliary cavalry unit. The tribesmen were stunned by the swiftness of the new commander's retaliation, and after he had followed through as far as Anglesey there were very few stirrings from that quarter for some time.

An altar dedicated to the Emperor Caracalla, his mother Julia, and brother Geta. After Caracalla had murdered his brother and married his mother, Geta's name was erased from all such inscriptions.

The colonnade in front of the granaries at Corstopitum. Below the stone-flagged floors were channels for the circulation of air to keep the grain dry.

Now it was the turn of the north. In a series of annual campaigns Agricola, having taken precautionary measures against the Brigantes, pushed back the northern boundary until he had claimed southern Scotland up to the neck of land between Forth and Clyde. He even penetrated beyond that to the Tay and set up a number of marching camps and signal stations. The fleet mounted devastating raids behind Caledonian lines; and he sailed vessels right round Britain to prove that it truly was an island.

With Lowland Scotland subdued for the time being, and a resounding defeat inflicted on a Highland army at Mons Graupius, somewhere near Inverness, permanent stability could still not be guaranteed without deploying larger forces than

Rome was willing to commit to the province. Security of a chosen demarcation line was the best that could be hoped for, no matter how much Agricola might long to complete his annexation of every last square mile.

To supply his forward outposts he built a fort and depot at Corstopitum (Corbridge) in Northumberland on Dere Street, the military highway leading from York through Catterick and across the Tyne gap to the slopes of the Cheviots. From its western gate he laid down another road, guarded by a sequence of intermediate forts, which the Anglo-Saxons were to dub Stanegate – a variant of many Stane or Stone Streets in England. There is some doubt as to whether Agricola himself carried this

*The Corbridge Lion, a local Romano-British sculptor's
conception of a lion devouring a stag.*

Just when Agricola had most reason to feel
pleased with his achievements and to hope for
suitable recognition, his British garrisons were
drained to provide reinforcements on the Continent
against invaders from Dacia – what is now Romania
and part of Hungary. Unable to pursue the conquest
of Scotland, he was in fact compelled to abandon
much of what he had won. The jealous Emperor
Domitian recalled him, not only not granting him
the Triumph or flamboyant victory parade usually
accorded to successful generals but ordering him to
enter Rome after nightfall so that there should be no

route to its obvious goal at Carlisle, but around AD
100 Trajan was to add more forts and probably
ensure that the road was serviceable as far as the
Solway.

Corbridge was occupied in its earliest phase by a
vexillation, or infantry detachment, posted from a
legion for special duties, together with a cavalry
wing of about 500 men. A tombstone in Hexham
abbey church shows a standard-bearer of this unit,
probably filched from a cemetery near the fort, as so
many things were over the ages.

While acquiring the hitherto unstable regions of
the north, Agricola kept a wary eye on Britons to his
rear. It was during his governorship that the most
marked strides in Romanization were made
throughout the province. Believing as much in
wooing the subject races as in coercing them,
Agricola put an end to civic corruption and profit-
eering by such functionaries as the *conductores* who
assessed and collected taxes, and who had too
frequently collected bribes on the side. He encouraged the education of the more amenable
natives into Roman ways, and threw his personal
and official influence behind civic amenities such as
town halls, bath-houses, public meeting-places, and
temples. Tribal dignitaries were coaxed by the
carrot of eventual full Roman citizenship into
devoting more time to efficient local administration.
Native craftsmen found themselves in favour
because of Agricola's flattering 'preference for British natural ability over the studied skill of the
Gauls', as Tacitus puts it.

*A tombstone in Hexham Abbey of Flavinus, standard-
bearer of the cavalry regiment Petriana, promoted to
the rank of centurion.*

The vicar's pele tower at Corbridge, a protection against Border raiders, built of stones from Corstopitum.

Remains of the fort established early in the fourth century around what is now Piercebridge.

public demonstration whatsoever. Instead of glory and promotion, Agricola had to pass his remaining years in discreet seclusion. Unlike modern superannuated commanders, he was unable to make a fortune out of selling his slanted memoirs to the Sunday newspapers; but his son-in-law Tacitus did his best to make up the deficiency by writing a fulsome and loyally selective biography.

Agricola's legacy was a network of roads serving some 60 or 70 guardian forts and allowing swift movement of troops. They also contributed to the expansion of trade and the easing of contacts between farms, mines, industrial centres and their markets. Although farmers were persuaded into compliance with new distribution and tax systems, new techniques were neither forced on them nor too readily explored. The rectangular plots known as Celtic fields went on being worked according to pre-Roman traditions within their lynchets – embankments formed by stones and spoil thrown up when clearing the ground. Such a field layout, lasting through and beyond Roman times, can still be seen above Grassington in Wharfedale.

What the Romans did take over for themselves, here as elsewhere, were the mineral deposits. Rich veins of lead through Shropshire, Derbyshire and the Yorkshire Dales were worked from opencast mines or deeper diggings. Lead 'pigs' dated from AD 81 have been found on Greenhow Hill to the east of Grassington, and other dated ingots have shown up in Swaledale. At Gargrave near Skipton there was a Roman-style house of some distinction that is unlikely to have been a farming villa: it could, however, have been the residence of some high-ranking official of the local mining industry. Similar quarters have been identified at Winterton and Roxby in Humberside as homes of imperial estate overseers or native entrepreneurs with leases from the government.

In the Peak District of Derbyshire the extraction of ore from 'rakes' or veins in the limestone was supervised from a place recorded as Lutudarum, with ingot marks of LVT, LVTVD, or LVTVDARES. This may have been Matlock or Wirksworth, both of which remained important mining towns through many centuries, or even Chesterfield. The 'Roman galleries' of the Masson and Rutland caverns at Matlock Bath are accessible to the interested visitor, who may well shudder at the thought of chipping a way through the square-cut passages 2 ft wide and 3 ft high (61 by 92 cm). Even the 'coffin' type galleries, 4 to 5 ft (1.2 to 1.5 m) high and some 100 ft (31 m) in length, are hardly inviting.

Matlock Bath provided its workers and, most probably, legionaries on leave with thermal waters for bathing or imbibing. It was less frequented, though, than Aquae Arnemetiae (Buxton) to the north-west. Like those at Bath, Buxton's medicinal springs were linked with religious observances; and, as with Bath, the patron deity was Celtic and feminine – the river goddess Arnemetia.

After Agricola's abrupt departure from Britain there followed three decades covered by only the flimsiest records. All we can deduce is that there was a renewal of strife all over the north of the province. Brigantian splinter groups ran wild again. Defences along the Caledonian border were breached. Such

chaos ensued that provincial governors during those 30-odd years seem to have lost any grip on what was going on. In Trajan's time an attempt was made to secure a frontier withdrawn as far back as the Stanegate, but this too was under constant threat from the north and from marauders south of the holding line. By AD 122 things had become so anarchic that the emperor Hadrian decided to come for a personal inspection; and the new governor, Aulus Platorus Nepos, brought in the Sixth Legion to replace the Ninth at York.

The emplacements and dispersions of the legions and their auxiliaries make a story as tangled as any deployments of the First or Second World War. From Hadrian's time onwards there were to be three full legions resident in Britain, amounting with their auxiliaries to more than 5000 men each. Vexillations or specialized groups were sent on detachment for

Hard Knott Castle, an early second-century fort, at the head of Eskdale, 800 ft (243 m) above sea level.

The station of Galava, on the outskirts of Ambleside above Lake Windermere.

specific duties, and frequently left their inscriptions – graffiti or solemn dedicatory stones – where they had carried out their tasks. Men from Syria, Spain and Turkey found themselves guarding the Tyne, the Forth, and the Clyde. Gauls and Teutons were pressed into service against or alongside Britons. At the same time, in a 'divide and rule' sort of exchange, levies of Britons were dispatched to fight on behalf of Rome along the Danube. But throughout the years of greatest influence, through all the comings and goings, the major battalions in Britannia were those of the Second Legion at Caerleon, the Twentieth at Chester, and the Sixth at York.

So we find ourselves facing a great historical mystery which has passed into legend and become the source of any number of essays, articles and novels. To make way for the Sixth Legion, the Ninth must have been evacuated from York and sent off to some prescribed destination. Perhaps it was for action against the Caledonians, for engineering work on new defences, or possibly for Continental service. But, having departed, they disap-

peared. No word of the legion as a whole was ever again reliably recorded. Fleeting mention of a few survivors has proved unhelpful. No trace of corpses, standards or equipment has ever been excavated, and nothing has been heard of their engagement in any major battle. Is there something in the suggestion that somehow, somewhere, they disgraced themselves so irreparably that all reference to their existence was expunged and the wretched survivors were divided up among other formations?

Whatever may have happened to the Ninth, the job of their successors was plain to Hadrian. To supplement the Dere Street bridge over the Tyne at Corstopitum a new one was built some miles to the east and named Pons Aelius in honour of the emperor, Publius Aelius Hadrianus. From its environs, today the city of Newcastle upon Tyne, there was to be a wall which would confirm Roman rather than Brigantian power 'from sea to sea', or at least ensure that tides of invasion flooding into the province from the barbarian north could be more effectively dammed.

The bath at Ravenglass in Cumbria, a naval base manned for defence against Irish raiders.

PLACES TO VISIT

Aldborough, North Yorkshire
Angle of town wall and mosaic pavements. Site museum.

Almondbury, West Yorkshire
Castle Hill fort of the Brigantes. SE 152140, by unclassified road off A616 2 miles (3.2 km) S of Huddersfield.

Bainbridge, North Yorkshire
Fort of *Virosidum* on mound above Wensleydale, on the Roman road of Craven's Way from Lancaster. SD 937901, off A684 at Bainbridge.

Corbridge, Northumberland
Foundations of legionary fortress and later ordnance depot for Hadrian's Wall. (*See also chapter on Hadrian's Wall.*)

Grassington, North Yorkshire
200-acre (80.9-ha) Romano-British 'Celtic field' system. SE 004651, 1½ miles (2.4 km) N of Grassington on B6265, 12 miles (19.2 km) N of Skipton.

Hard Knott Castle, Cumbria
Substantial fort remains and parade ground. NY 218014, beside unclassified road through Hard Knott Pass 8 miles (12.8 km) NE of Ravenglass.

Hexham, Northumberland
The Manor Office of the Moot Hall built almost entirely of Roman stones from Corbridge. Abbey crypt has many Roman stones with dedicatory inscriptions to Septimius Severus, the god Apollo, and others. Bowl of the font carved from base of a Roman pillar. In the south transept a tombstone to Flavius, a cavalry standard-bearer.

Ingleborough Hill, North Yorkshire
Brigantian hill-fort with ruined walls of millstone grit slabs. SD 741745, 2000 ft (608 m) above B6255 3 miles (4.8 km) NE of Ingleton.

Malton, North Yorkshire
Roman museum in market-place with pottery, stone and glass from Malton fort and town. On A64 18 miles (28.8 km) NE of York.

Matlock Bath, Derbyshire
Roman lead-mine galleries in Masson and Rutland caverns.

Piercebridge, Co. Durham
Fourth-century fort wall and remains of gateways. Remains of Roman bridge uncovered in 1972.

Rey Cross, Co. Durham
Marching camp near Roman road. NY 901124, off A66 9 miles (14.4 km) W of Barnard Castle.

Ribchester, Lancashire
Fort granaries. Site museum. SD 650350, on B6245 3 miles (4.8 km) SW of Longridge.

Scarborough, North Yorkshire
Signal station on cliff near Scarborough castle, one of a chain to co-ordinate land and sea defences against Saxon intruders.

Stanwick, North Yorkshire
Brigantian fortifications. NZ 180115, by B6274 7 miles (11.2 km) N of Richmond.

Wheeldale Moor, North Yorkshire
'Wade's Causeway', section of Roman road from Whitby to Malton. SE 812988 to SE 793938, off unclassified road 2 miles (3.2 km) S of Goathland railway station.

Whitley Castle, Northumberland
Ditch defences of second-century fort rebuilt in third century. NY 696487, off A689 2 miles (3.2 km) NW of Alston.

York, North Yorkshire
Sections of Roman walls below medieval walls, especially clear between Multangular Tower and St Leonard's Hospital. Fragment of Roman street and pillar in cellar of the Treasurer's House, Chapter House Street, *National Trust*. Roman Bath Inn, St Sampson's Square, has remains of baths and hypocaust. Yorkshire Museum in Museum Street has busts and statues including those of Constantine the Great and Mars, and local archaeological collections. Fortress walls in Museum Gardens.

Hadrian's Wall at Walltown Crags, Northumberland.

HADRIAN'S WALL

THE first phase of building the great barrier from east to west took about four years. It extended over 80 Roman miles (about 73 of our own miles, 117 km) and took advantage of every natural feature to command clear views of likely enemy approaches. Hadrian did not stay to supervise the work but left definitive instructions for its progress. From east of Newcastle to Gilsland there was to be a solid stone wall, continued thereafter by turf because of the dearth of good local stone in the west. Garrisons would be accommodated in the Agricolan forts already spaced out along the Stanegate to the rear.

By the time a long sweep of stone defences had been completed it was evident that certain amendments would be desirable. To speed up construction and economize on materials, the prescribed thickness of 10 ft (3 m) was reduced to 8 ft (2.4 m) though where lower parts had already been built to the 10-ft (3-m) standard, the reduced gauge was simply added on top. It was also realized that lookout towers and forts were essential on the actual line of the wall, portions of which had to be chipped out to allow for these insertions. Fortlets known as milecastles at intervals of a Roman mile housed complements of up to 50 men. Between each two milecast-

This relief shows soldiers building turf and stone fortifications.

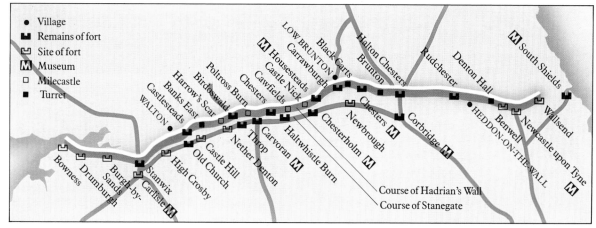

Key positions along Hadrian's Wall.

les were two evenly spaced signal turrets. Larger forts at strategic points had barracks for up to 1000 troops each. The turf embankment beyond Gilsland began with fortlets of earth and timber, gradually replaced by stone. Beyond the end of the Wall proper at Bowness a number of mile-fortlets and watchtowers were spaced out for a further 40 miles (65 km) down the Cumbrian coast, but not joined by a wall.

There were two accompanying ditches: one about 25 ft (7.3 m) wide and of varying depth immediately in front of the Wall, and behind the Wall a similar ditch known as the Vallum with mounds 10 ft (3 m) high along either side. This rear ditch marked the administrative boundary of the province and also served to protect the backs of the defenders from the unreliable Brigantes, part of whose territory in fact stretched beyond the Wall.

All construction work was done by legionary engineers, but the garrisons were supplied by auxiliaries under Roman officers. As was the practice in such situations, most of them came from other parts of the Empire: the Wall is rich in the inscriptions of legions which built it and cohorts which served along it. Gods, wives and official benefactors are all celebrated in these memorials. Only in later stages do we find British recruits appearing in the border defence contingents.

Hadrian's adopted son and successor, Antoninus Pius, found himself faced by renewed belligerence from the Picts and Scots, and decided to move troops forward to a shorter defence line used previously by Agricola. The main strongpoints along Hadrian's Wall were evacuated in favour of a new turf rampart on a stone foundation between Forth and Clyde, known to us as the Antonine Wall. It did not serve its purpose for long. The forts were inadequate for the garrisons required, and some time after AD 158 it became necessary to fall back on Hadrian's Wall. Evidence of the Antonine Wall's full history is scanty, but obviously there were phases of occupation, abandonment, and reoccupation over some 40 years.

In AD 197 the provincial governor Clodius Albinus withdrew most of his armies from Britain to fight in his bid to become absolute emperor, instead of merely joint ruler with Lucius Septimius Severus. Enemies from the north seized the opportunity to break through the Wall and devastate northern England. When Severus had defeated Albinus and thrown his corpse to the dogs, he set about subduing eastern countries before turning west to tackle the upheaval in Britain. For a while he allowed his newly appointed governor to buy off the tribesmen, but in AD 208 came personally to drive them back into Scotland. Hadrian's original fortifications had fallen into such disrepair that Severus had to put in hand a major restoration; and we should probably give him greater credit than Hadrian for the Wall as we know it.

While in Britain he learned of his son's intention of murdering him and replacing him, and although this plot was foiled he fell into a state of acute depression, exacerbated by chronic gout. In AD 211 he died at York after a session of over-eating which some of his contemporaries said was a suicide attempt. Soon afterwards the Caledonian campaigns were once more given up, and the border defences lay once more along Hadrian's Wall.

Severus had introduced a number of reforms into

military life which made that life a lot more agreeable for regular soldiers. Hitherto it had been forbidden for any man to marry during the 25 years of his service. Now such marriages were allowed, and wives and families could be installed in the *vicus* which invariably grew up around a fort. Some renovated forts were provided with married quarters. Leases of land were granted to soldiers against their retirement, and units tended to stay where they were instead of being frequently posted to new theatres of action or remoter garrisons. They raised families and probably put some to work on their plot of land, some into apprenticeships or shops in the civilian settlement. All this kept burning a stronger desire to protect their environment against intruders.

The modern traveller along the Wall will find evocative remains of civilized living quarters, personal relics and dedications, and bath-houses where men and, judging by the profusion of combs and hairpins found there, women met to bathe and gossip. All this stands out so much more sharply when seen against the wild background of hills and rock, the steely loughs, and the vast sky; and always there is the eerie rustling and moaning of the wind, sometimes rising to a howl like some barbaric battle-cry.

Starting from the eastern tip of the defence line, even beyond so-called Wallsend, we find there was a Hadrianic fort at South Shields which by the time of Severus had become a supply base, its 20 granaries and other storehouses backing up the renewed advance into Scotland. The site of the fort can be traced in the Roman Remains Park.

A few yards of the Wall itself were extracted from the Swan Hunter shipyard in Wallsend at the beginning of this century. Some of it travelled further than Hadrian could ever have dreamed, displayed in a glass case aboard the ocean liner *Carpathia*, which came from these shipyards.

Benwell was once a station for a cavalry troop. Three stones before the fort gateway mark the end of a causeway across the Vallum, most of which was filled in as the civilian settlement took over from the military. A regional god, Antenociticus, was worshipped in a nearby temple whose toothy remains jut incongruously from the garden of a modern house. One of the deity's altars was erected by a cavalry officer celebrating his promotion to the rank of *quaestor*, a privileged combination of army paymaster and tax collector.

The tombstone of Regina of the Catuvellauni at South Shields fort, far from her Hertfordshire base.

Heading westwards, the first visible piece of Wall is to be found by the A69 at Denton Burn, with a fragment of turret, soon to be followed by a 100-yard segment at Heddon-on-the-Wall. There are also broken gashes of the northern ditch and the Vallum, becoming more regular when the road starts to ride along the buried wall itself.

This obliteration of the original stones was ordered as a result of yet another invasion from Scotland. When the Young Pretender led his troops into Carlisle and prepared to march deep into England, Field-Marshal Wade and his government forces were on the far side of the country in Newcastle. Upon receiving news of Carlisle's surrender he set off to retake it, but the snow and mud were so appalling that he got no farther than Hexham, by which time a thousand of his men were

A head of Antenociticus from Benwell, where this Celtic god was a local cult figure.

sick and unfit for action. Ultimately the Jacobites were defeated, but the lesson had been learned: in case of future unrest there had to be a reliable east-to-west highway. Hadrian's engineers had obligingly provided a suitable foundation running straight and true for many miles, and this was appropriated without any concern for historical or archaeological niceties. Known as the Military Road – not to be confused with the Military Way which had served as a Roman supply road south of the Wall – this new construction made havoc of Rudchester fort and its Mithraic temple before heading along the route of the modern B6318 to the Portgate crossroads with Dere Street (the A68) and on beyond Chollerford Bridge to where at last the Wall breaks free again. Towards its farther extremity there was vandalism in our own time: during the Second World War an urgent demand for road metal led to the destruction of over 300 yd (274 m) of Wall near Greenhead.

South of the Portgate junction, Corstopitum was given a new lease of life around AD 140. Hadrian had not included the deserted fort in his basic scheme, preferring one at Hunnum (Haltonchesters), now

The crossing of the vallum *at the entrance to Benwell cavalry fort.*

flattened and overplanted by later generations of farmers. But when Antoninus Pius decided on the renewal of operations in Scotland, Corbridge was brought back into service as an ordnance depot with the equivalent of R.E. and R.E.M.E. workshops. A civilian settlement with smiths, potters, tanners, merchants and retailers grew up around it. Even when campaigns against Scotland were called off, the fortress remained healthy and is known to have done brisk business with Greek and other merchants from the Middle East. An uncompleted army storehouse was converted by civilians into shops, and the town became a trading centre for iron and lead from mines in the region. Suffering from barbarian raids in the middle of the fourth century, it was rebuilt by the governor-general Theodosius with protective ramparts; but by then the end was only a few decades away.

From a slope above the North Tyne, Brunton turret looks down on the massive stones of a bridge abutment at Cilurnum (Chesters). The first bridge here carried the walkway of the Wall across the river, later replaced by a wider structure to carry the Military Way also. Pier foundations of this can be

A fragment of wall and turret, enclosing an altar, at Brunton, above the Military Road where it descends to the river Tyne crossing near Chollerford Bridge.

seen when the water is low. To guard the far bank there was originally another turret, but it was soon decided that a more substantial fort was necessary at such a key crossing. A cavalry fort covering almost six acres was established with a large headquarters building, a luxurious house for the officer com-

The entrance to the aerarium *or strongroom below the headquarters building at Chesters.*

manding complete with central heating and a private bath suite, barrack blocks, and garrison bath-houses outside the main enclosure. Muddled records of the fort's existence had at one time been interpreted as indicating that the stables had been built underground, and when the entrance to a subterranean chamber was found it was assumed that this would lead to them. Instead, an iron-studded oak door proved to be that of a strong-room, containing coins dating mainly from the time of Severus.

The owner of Chesters manor house through a large part of the nineteenth century was the historian John Clayton. His property included four of the Wall forts, and he was enlightened enough to ensure that they and neighbouring stretches of Wall were no longer raided for building stone. He personally excavated some of the local sites, including Chesters fort, and founded the museum here.

At Brocolitia (Carrawburgh) is the mound of a station built as an afterthought, to fill the dangerously wide gap between Chesters and the next large garrison at Housesteads. Not far from it is the outline of a Mithraeum, provided with replicas of original altars now given sanctuary within a reconstruction of the temple in Newcastle Museum of Antiquities. On the left of the entrance to the site is a hearth for preparing food, close to which was the ceremonial pit in which neophytes had to undergo their initiation ordeal. In the sanctuary, the three main altars all bore dedications by officers from the fort.

Another deity worshipped at this spot was Coventina, into whose well the devout tossed nearly 14,000 coins, to be recovered in Victorian times. Of these, 300 are brass coins commemorating defeat of the Brigantes by Antoninus Pius and showing Britannia with her head bowed.

The apodyterium *or disrobing room of the regimental bath-house at Chesters.*

The temple of Mithras, Carrawburgh, containing copies of the original altars preserved in Newcastle upon Tyne.

HOUSESTEADS

Hadrian's Wall   Workshops   Store   Commander's house   Granaries   Via Principalis   Via Praetoria   Water tank

West Gate   Barracks   Via Decumana   Hospital   Headquarters   North Gate   South Gate   Latrines   East Gate

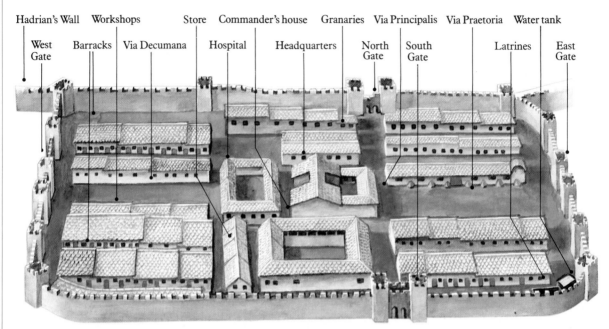

An impression of the fort at Housesteads on the Whin Sill, an outcrop of igneous rock forming a natural defence.

Communal latrines – these had a constant supply of fresh water to cleanse the sponges which the legionaries used before the advent of toilet paper.

The northern gateway to the fort, which was designed to hold 1000 troops.

Surely the most impressive fortress in dimensions and in its setting on a sheer rocky outcrop is Vercovicium (Housesteads), with well-preserved gateways, barrack blocks, granaries, commandant's house, a treasury, and latrines designed to follow the slope of the land, supplied by ducts from a stone cistern. Among the cavalrymen known to have served here were 1000 of a Tungrian cohort from a *civitas* by the river Maas in what is now Belgium. During their occupancy a civilian settlement flourished, accommodating veterans who had married women from the neighbouring hills and valleys. Among its buildings was a tavern, buried under whose floors have been found the skeletons of a man and woman, with a knife or sword point buried in the man's ribs. One wonders what drunken brawl, possibly brought on by jealousy, led to this killing.

Housesteads is a fine place from which to set out on a walk along the Wall. Westwards there is a firm footpath along the actual stones, snaking and lunging its way over the crags towards a milecastle. Cuddy's Crags offer spectacular vistas in all directions, and then one can descend to the junction of the Pennine Way with the Wall. Another climb above a lough leads to a dip in the hills and the squat foundation of a milecastle known as Castle Nick. The highest point in the Wall is at the breathtaking summit of Winshield Crags.

The view eastwards from Housesteads milecastle,

looking back along the ridge towards the fort.

A couple of miles to the rear of the Wall lies Vindolanda (Chesterholm), where the Stanegate crosses a stream at a point marked by a tall cylindrical Roman milestone still in its original position. The base of another stands slightly less than a Roman mile to the west. Vindolanda was one of Agricola's Stanegate fortifications, later reinforced to back up the resources of the Wall. In modern times a reconstruction of a turret and section of Wall has been set on the slope above the remains of the *vicus.*

A turret. The front of this would be built flush into the Wall, two storeys high.

A milecastle, housing between 25 and 50 men. North and south gateways controlled movement through the Wall.

A reconstructed section of wall and turret at Chesterholm.

This domestic scene on a tombstone from Murrell Hill, Cumbria, shows a lady with a fan and her pet bird.

An inscription from High Rochester, which declares: 'A detachment of the Twentieth Legion Valeria and Victrix made this.' The boar lying between Mars and Hercules is the legion's symbol.

This ivory knife handle in the shape of a gladiator was found at South Shields fort.

A Roman Army Museum has been opened at Banna (Carvoran), once the base of a detachment of Syrian archers. One tombstone found here was dedicated by a centurion of a Dalmatian contingent to the 'Divine Manes of Aurelia Faia', his 'most holy wife who lived 33 years without blemish'. *Manes* signified 'the good' and was generally applied to souls which, having departed from the body, watched over burial grounds and monuments. There was also an altar dedicated to one of Hadrian's adopted sons, Lucius Aelius Caesar, by a prefect worried by a vision and praying for his patron's safety – a plea which failed to work, since Lucius soon proved unfit for high office and was driven to take poison, leaving the imperial succession to the other adopted son, Antoninus Pius.

In 1915 a postman delivering to a nearby farmhouse tugged at what he thought was the rim of an old bucket embedded in the earth, to find that it was a bronze measuring pot for corn, now on show in the museum at Chesters.

Where the Wall reaches the river Irthing are chunks of bridge pier and abutment. Gilsland's old vicarage has a stretch of wide stone base topped by a narrower upper section, and turrets and a milecastle crown one tract leading to the walls and gateways of the fort at Camboglanna (Birdoswald). Beyond the Irthing we are soon in less rocky country, but the Wall pursues its course marked by turrets and a signal tower until we are left with little more than the earthworks of the ditch and Vallum. Carlisle is still a walled town, but the walls are no longer Roman. At Stanwix on its northern fringe was once a huge fortress of which nothing now remains.

The western extremity of the Wall straggles through Burgh-by-Sands, where Edward I was to die after his own efforts against the Scots, and Drumburgh, where Roman stones were quarried for a castle in the time of Henry VIII, and peters out at Maia (Bowness). Here the tides have undermined a large part of the fort, leaving only a few traces on the hill now crowned by the church. Down the Cumbrian coast from here were the outriders of fortlet and signal station through Beckfoot, Maryport and Workington, ever watchful for seaborne raiders from Scotland or Ireland.

North of the Wall, even when ventures into the heart of Caledonia had been repulsed or abandoned for one reason or another, a few perilously exposed strongholds were maintained. Two roads had been laid into those contested regions: the Devil's Causeway to Berwick and, linked with it by a lateral road from Whittingham to High Rochester, the much more important Dere Street from Corbridge over the Cheviots and into the Eildon Hills. Beside this thoroughfare were set up marching camps and permanent forts.

The little village school at Rochester, by the scenic route to the summit of Carter Bar, has become a private house but retains the school porch built entirely of stones from the fort of Bremenium (High Rochester). Two round stones at the corners were in fact *ballista* shot. Not far from the church is a camp which was constructed as only a temporary measure but must have been large enough to hold a full legion, and outlived many of its supposedly more durable contemporaries. High Rochester was one of Agricola's most important outposts, beginning with a turf rampart later strengthened with stone. Even after the line of the Antonine Wall had been relinquished and Hadrian's Wall reinvigorated, it remained of great tactical value and is known to have functioned until at least the middle of the fourth century. It is renowned for its *ballistae* platforms, set up by a vexillation from the Twentieth Legion who have left a carved advertisement of their accomplishment, flanked by crude carvings of Mars and Hercules. Smaller earthworks in the vicinity come within modern army firing ranges.

Outside the main fort is the base of a circular tomb opened in 1850 by a Revenue officer stationed in this remote place to pounce on whisky smugglers from across the border. A couple of adjacent rectangular tombs were later ravaged to provide stones for a sheep-pen.

Right on the Anglo-Scottish border, some 1400 ft (427 m) above sea level, are strewn the camps and fortlets of Chew Green, described by Sir Nikolaus Pevsner as 'the most remarkable visible group of Roman earthworks in Britain'. It seems appropriate

A sesterce of Hadrian, found in the river Tyne.

A large bronze head of the Emperor Hadrian, rediscovered in the river Thames near London Bridge.

that they should be reached today from a modern military road through Redesdale Camp, open to the public when the red flags are not flying to warn of firing on the range; or there is a route along the Pennine Way from Byrness. Set slightly below the crown of the ridge, Chew Green had its own sentinel in the form of a signal station with a good view to the north. On Dere Street nearby are stone sockets for what may have been signposts, known as the Outer Golden Pot and the Inner Golden Pot, two of several which are known to have existed in the neighbourhood.

Hadrian's Wall was overrun in 197, 296, and 367. The hurried patching-up by Theodosius around 369 was the last serious attempt to keep it operative. By the end of the fourth century there were not enough trained men to defend it, and not enough Roman officers left to train replacements.

PLACES TO VISIT

Carlisle, Cumbria
Museum of regional archaeology in Tullie House, Castle Street.

Hadrian's Wall forts and stations
Near Heddon-on-the-Wall the B6138 leaves east-bound A69 from Newcastle to run along the Wall. From side lanes or within easy walking distance the following suggested features may be visited (in east–west sequence).

Chesters cavalry fort and bridge. Site museum.

Carrawburgh fort mound, Mithraeum, and Coventina's Well.

Housesteads fortress. Site museum.

Chesterholm – remains of Vindolanda, and reconstruction of turret. Site museum.

Roman Army Museum at Carvoran.

Turrets at Denton Hall; Brunton, above Chollerford Bridge; Black Carts; Banks East.

Milecastles at Castle Nick; Cawfields; Poltross Burn; and Harrow's Scar.

Newcastle upon Tyne, Tyne & Wear
Museum of Antiquities, University Quadrangle, with history of Hadrian's Wall in models, plans, photographs and reconstructions.

Rochester, Northumberland
One-time village school with ballista stones on porch. Roman fort of *Bremenium* with ballista platforms at High Rochester. On A68 (Dere Street) 5 miles (8 km) NW of Otterburn.

South Shields, Tyne & Wear
Sections of fort and granaries in Roman Remains Park, Baring Street. Site museum.

A brass sesterce *showing Hadrian on the obverse and a saddened Britannia on the reverse, her head resting on her hand.*

The twin towers of Reculver, Kent, which stand above a fragmentary Fort of the Saxon Shore.

DECLINE AND DEPARTURE

THE *pax Romana*, that Roman peace traditionally assumed to have prevailed for unbroken
centuries, was in reality an uneasy peace at the
best of times. Often disrupted not only by inrushes
of predatory barbarians but by the quarrels and
ambitions of its rulers, it had much in common with
Hadrian's Wall – sometimes presenting an impreg-
nable front, sometimes breached and partially demolished by enemies, shored up again, then weake-
ned by uncertainties from within. Emperors assassinated their rivals or were assassinated by them.
Many killed off members of their own family if they
doubted their loyalty. Armies were withdrawn from
embattled frontiers to back up campaigns of personal rather than national glory. A period of relative
tranquillity could be shattered by some egotist's
greed; and the cost of restoring that tranquillity was
often heavy.

Events in Britain mirrored events in the Empire.
Spurts of aggression from the north were followed
by consolidation of defence lines, some decades of
peaceful development on farms and in border settlements, and then periods of hesitancy and piecemeal
withdrawal. As Agricola had discovered, full-time
investment of hostile territory required more troops
on a permanent basis than could ever be spared from
other European trouble spots; and any removal of
defensive units was inevitably the signal for renewed assaults.

After the punitive measures of Septimius Severus
there came one of the longest periods of peace, in
spite of his son Caracalla's decision to abandon most
of what had been won in Scotland. But a threat was
building up from another direction.

Severus had divided the country between two
governors to lessen the chances of any repetition of a
stab at seizing the throne such as Clodius Albinus
had made. When Diocletian became emperor in AD
284 and delegated personal responsibilities by
elevating a trusted friend to the shared honour of
Augustus and appointing two subordinate Caesars,
he also sub-divided Britain still further. There were
now four provinces: Britannia Prima, Britannia
Secunda, Maxima Caesariensis and Flavia Caesariensis; and some while later, after his reign, a fifth
was created with the name Valentia, which may have
covered North Wales. Two appointments were
made of senior military officers, one to control the
north, the other a special fleet commander with
wide-ranging powers to deal as he thought best with
the Saxon pirates plaguing the sea lanes between
Britain and Gaul.

The methods of this naval patrol commander,
Carausius, soon came under suspicion. He used his
unique position to fill his own pockets: slyly allowing raiders to pillage the coast, he would descend on
their ships only when they were fully laden with
loot, and help himself to it. It was also rumoured
that he made cynical deals with the raiders, to their
mutual profit. Swollen with pride, he then decided
to supplant Diocletian's joint ruler Maximian, rallied the fleet to his cause, and proclaimed himself
Emperor Marcus Aurelius Mauseaeus Carausius.
Maximian's attempt to nip this insubordination in
the bud by sending a loyal naval squadron against

*Two gold coins of successive usurpers, both minted in
London. Above: The* aureus *of Carausius. Below: The*
aureus *of Allectus, with the standing armed figure of Mars
on the reverse.*

- ■ Provincial capitals
- □ Bishoprics
- ● Cantonal capitals or main administrative centres

0 10 20 30 40 50 miles

0 20 40 60 80 kilometres

HADRIAN'S WALL

● Carlisle ● Corbridge

BRITANNIA SECUNDA

● Aldborough

□ **York**

● Chester

□ **Lincoln**

R. TRENT

FLAVIA CAESARIENSIS

● Wroxeter ● Leicester ● Caistor

● Chesterton

R. SEVERN

MAXIMA CAESARIENSIS

● Colchester

● Gloucester

■ **Cirencester** ● St Albans

R. THAMES ◻ **London**

● Silchester

● Canterbury

BRITANNIA PRIMA

● Winchester

● Chichester

● Exeter ● Dorchester

The four provincial divisions established in the late third century.

him failed because of bad weather. For seven years Carausius enjoyed his regal splendour, took over the running of Britain and a part of Gaul around Boulogne, and had his own coins struck.

Also, to guard against reprisals from Rome, he set about building a chain of defences along the Litus Saxonicum, referred to by historians as the Forts of the Saxon Shore. These watched over the coastline from Brancaster in Norfolk through Burgh, Bradwell, Reculver, Richborough, Dover, Lympne, and Pevensey, to Portchester in Hampshire. Some were adaptations of earlier forts such as the old bases at Richborough and Dover. Others were new.

The spell of grandeur could not last. After his Boulogne base had been repossessed by Constantius Chlorus, Carausius was assassinated by his own procurator, Allectus, who assumed the imperial titles for himself. These he enjoyed for three years before Constantius struck again, this time launching a fleet against the English coast and overthrowing the pretender.

While these bids for power were being made and unmade, the Saxon menace had not abated. At the same time the Picts were taking advantage of the absence of a garrison from Hadrian's Wall, which soon had to be extensively repaired by Constantius Chlorus. Scots from Ireland intensified raids along the western coast until in the fifth century they turned their attention to carving a kingdom out of Pictish territory and in due course imposed their name on it.

It is thought to have been in the time of Constantine that the military commanders of north and south were designated Dux Britanniarum, Duke of the Britons, and Comes Litoris Saxonici, Count of the Saxon Shore. Both had unenviable tasks. Picts, Scots and Saxons were co-ordinating their offensives against the Roman-held lands. There were repeated attacks on the Wall and civilian settlements, which in AD 369 Theodosius found it necessary to convert into strongly fortified villages. Less than 20 years later another usurper, Magnus Maximus, serving as Dux Britanniarum and known to have been popular with his British troops, led a large proportion of them away to Gaul with the idea of marching on Rome itself. He succeeded in becoming Emperor of the West, and although his ambitions had left Britain unguarded, there were at first few of the expected repercussions. The Wall was ceasing to be a battleground as the northern tribes began to doubt the wisdom of their opportu-

nist alliance with the Saxons and saw that they had common cause with the Romano-Britons.

Some folk beyond the border had already made their peace with the northern administration and entered service as *foederati* – allied auxiliaries who enjoyed the perks of the Romanized way of life. Attempts were made to pacify intruders in the south by enlisting them also as *foederati*, giving grants of land and housing to Angles and Saxons if they would serve alongside Romano-Britons in defence of their shared property. Some mercenaries played along; but when their numbers were large enough they showed signs of wanting to seize the reins for themselves.

Renewed attempts were made to thwart attacks from the east. Signal towers were set up on headlands along the Durham and Yorkshire coasts, including sites at Ravenscar, Goldsborough and Scarborough, working in conjunction with patrol vessels from the Tyne, Tees and Humber estuaries. Excavations at Huntcliff in Cleveland have shown that raiders knew the importance of these warning towers and sought to put them out of commission: here there had obviously been a skirmish, leaving behind it the skeletons of the defenders and their dog.

The forts of the Saxon Shore were strengthened to keep at bay the assailants from the Jutland and Rhineland areas, yet many of them were manned by

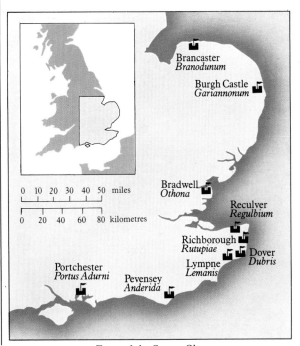

Forts of the Saxon Shore.

On the cliff edge near Scarborough Castle keep are the remains of a fourth-century signal station built to watch for seaborne raiders. It is believed to have been 100 ft (30 m) high.

mercenaries and shrewd collaborators from those same homelands, serving alongside native Britons but biding their time.

Nine of the forts have survived in varying states of preservation. Branodunum (Brancaster) on the north coast of Norfolk near the Wash has little to show, though excavation has confirmed that the fort covered more than 6 acres (3 h) and had walls 9 ft (2.7 m) thick. The next link in the chain, Gariannonum (Burgh Castle) close to the border of Norfolk and Suffolk, still thrusts three sides of its walled enclosure and mighty bastions up from the earth. Its fourth wall stood once on a cliff above the then much wider estuary of the rivers Yare and Waveney, with quays for patrol and supply ships. In Essex, Othona (Bradwell) is another fort which has wasted away over the centuries but at least has stretches of wall and a bastion to testify to its past importance, which is more than can be said for the fort which conceivably lay between it and Burgh.

In Roman records there are references to a place called Sitomagus which has never been satisfactorily identified. Common sense would indicate that it must have been sited in the otherwise wide and vulnerable gap between Burgh and Bradwell. There is thought to have been some sort of fortification near Felixstowe, but still there would have been the need for another on East Anglia's out-thrust into the sea. Trying to establish a possible location, we can trace an interesting convergence of three Roman roads: one from Coddenham in Suffolk via Yoxford, one from the Icenian capital at Caistor St Edmund, and a minor one in between. They have all been erased before reaching their destination; but that destination could be the Sitomagus declared by the *Antonine Itinerary*, a fourth-century road guide, to be 32 miles from Venta Icenorum (Caistor) – which is just what Dunwich in Suffolk is . . . or was. During Saxon and early medieval times this was England's main east coast sea-port, and maintained a body of

Burgh Castle in Norfolk, where a unit of the Stablesian cavalry from what is now Yugoslavia was stationed towards the end of the Roman occupation.

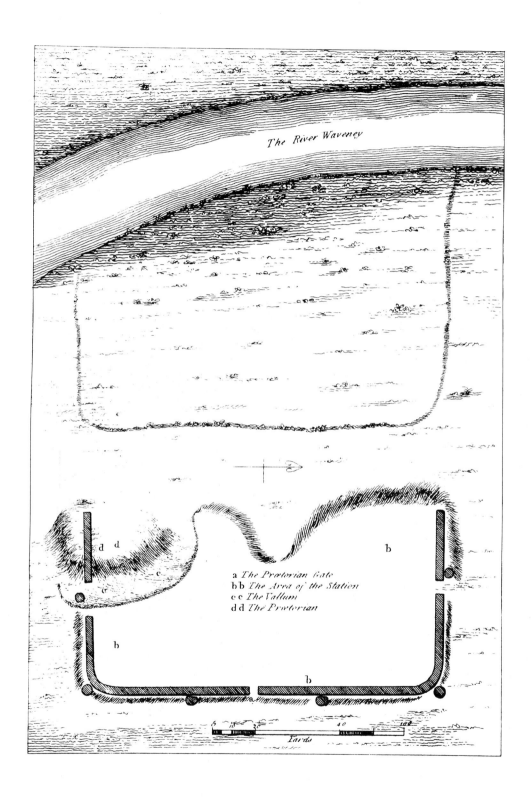

The River Waveney

a *The Prætorian Gate*
bb *The Area of the Station*
cc *The Vallum*
dd *The Prætorian*

Yards

An eighteenth-century plan of the remains of Burgh Castle above the river Waveney marshes.

royal galleys as large as that of London. It is unlikely that the Romans would have failed to utilize such a commanding position.

In 1754 the Suffolk historian Thomas Gardner wrote of inexplicably massive stones discovered after a severe gale, a circle of large stumps of piles, 'also a stone Coffin, wherein were human Bones covered with Tiles', and the 'Pipes of an Aqueduct, some of lead, others of gray Earth'. He also makes tantalizing references to a stone wall 'cemented exceeding strong' and 'several Pieces of old Coins'. The piles might have been those of a *pharos* or of a watchtower, or even part of a temple. But there is now no telling. Violent gales have destroyed all the churches and monastic buildings of old Dunwich; and out there below the water may also be the ruins of a great Roman station.

Regulbium (Reculver) was taken over by King Egbert of Kent as the site of a Saxon church, later supplied with twin towers which are still kept up as navigational landmarks. Such of the fort as Egbert and his successors failed to obliterate was eroded by nature, and now there are only a few relics of its full extent.

Rutupiae (Richborough), on the other hand, still has well over three-quarters of its original area exposed: the truncated edge now lies under the railway line. Aulus Plautius's bridgehead remained in uninterrupted use throughout the whole Roman occupation, and later provided the basis for the most impressive fortress of the Saxon Shore when its earthworks were replaced by huge stone walls. Towards the end, although Christianity was by now the official religion of the Empire, a pagan temple was built within the enclosure. The present site museum is a treasure-house of finds from every phase of Richborough's existence: weapons, harness, bronze busts, souvenirs of different emperors and commanders, and domestic items such as dice games and toilet sets.

A stretch of Burgh Castle's rubble wall with a facing of tiles and local flint.

The road over Blackstone Edge above Greater Manchester, with stone setts and

a trough into which a cart's brake-pole could grip on the steep descent.

THE MILDENHALL TREASURE

In 1942 ploughmen at West Row, near Mildenhall in Suffolk, unearthed a collection of tableware thought at first to be pewter and not officially reported until 1946. After heavy incrustation had been cleaned away the items were found to be of fourth-century silver in an excellent state of preservation, imported from Gaul, the Mediterranean, and the East, and were declared Treasure Trove. The hoard must have been buried by a well-to-do family threatened by Anglo-Saxon pillaging, and it has even been suggested that the owner of such rich imports might have been the Christian general Lupicinus whom the emperor Julian sent to stem the barbarian inroads but later arrested – before, perhaps, he could return to disinter his belongings.

The Great Dish, 2 ft (60.5 cm) across, with the head of Oceanus surrounded by a frieze of sea creatures.

A bowl with a domed lid, its knob in the form of a silver-gilt Triton blowing a conch shell.

Outer circle of the Great Dish, with Bacchus and Silenus.

A fluted bowl with two swing handles.

Dubris (Dover), as we have noted earlier, was built over long ago. Further round the curve of south-east Kent, the next fort was not buried but simply collapsed downhill. The tracts of Romney Marsh below it are thought to have been largely flooded at the time of the Roman invasion, forming a bay on whose edge an anchorage was established at Portus Lemanis (Lympne), with a guardian fort now known as Stutfall Castle. This was certainly strengthened in the fourth century, but its position could not have been very secure. Today the scattered blocks look from a distance like a flock of Romney Marsh sheep grazing at random on the hillside.

Anderida (Pevensey) in Sussex stood once on an uninhabited peninsula and, unlike many long-established forts, never acquired a considerable civilian settlement about its walls. Internal accommodation seems to have been on an emergency footing: makeshift huts from the time of Carausius were not detectably improved during the last vigils along the Saxon Shore. In spite of its formidable walls it could have offered little resistance to an onslaught in the late fifth century by the Saxon chieftain Aella and his sons who, according to the *Anglo-Saxon Chronicle*, 'slew all the inhabitants' so that 'there was not even one Briton left there'. Nineteenth-century excavations uncovered a deep well which contained *ballista* shot and a number of skulls – oddly, not those of defenders but of wolves. Subsequent digging located another well into which had been dropped a variety of items including leather sandals, the skull of a domestic cat, and the original bark strands of the well-rope. There were also seeds of plants such as flax, buttercup, henbane and vetch. Finds of this kind can be related to other analyses within the province. In recent years a cache of seeds in York provided evidence of plants which must have flourished there but in our own time cannot be found anywhere north of Huntingdon – an indication that the climate of northern England in Roman times was much milder than it is now.

Portchester came at the end of the protective belt. Its parapet walk is still there for those who wish to play at Romano-British sentry-go, and from those walls must have resounded hearty cheers, a thousand years later, when Henry V set sail with his armies for the humbling of the French at Agincourt.

But, sturdy as they were, the forts could not withstand the Angles and Saxons who came in like a slow, swirling tide, not directly undermining the coastal breakwaters but lapping round them, insinuating themselves, behaving sometimes as good neighbours and intermarrying with the Britons, asserting themselves only when it was clear that there would be no effective retaliation from Rome. At no time did one well-organized national army invade with the set purpose of sweeping the Britons out of their homesteads and taking over centralized administration of the province; but constant pressure from powerful groups made it clear to those Britons what their ultimate fate was likely to be.

Early in the fifth century the provincials who had been brought up in a Roman way of life and taught to rely on Roman protection appealed to the Emperor Honorius for just such protection. Their message arrived when the Goths were at the gates of Rome, and in AD 410 came the official write-off: local authorities were regretfully told that they must fend for themselves.

Contrary to the neatly packaged lessons of conventional English history, they did fend remarkably well for themselves over a couple of hundred years. The so-called Dark Ages began with a protracted twilight in which the Romano-British kept their torches burning with considerable courage, and from which there often seemed a chance of their emerging into a new dawn. Although by the middle of the fifth century a further appeal had been made to Rome on the grounds that 'the barbarians drive us to the sea, the sea drives us to the barbarians, and between these two means of death we are either slain or drowned', local chieftains still clung doggedly to the traditions in which they had been brought up. Some Britons gave up the struggle and fled into Wales, Cornwall or Britanny. Others pursued their livelihoods and went on decorating and extending their houses in the belief that things could not get *that* bad; and, when things too obviously worsened, hoped to fight off alien burglars and cattle rustlers by forming corps of local vigilantes.

The accredited bungler of the period was Vortigern, a 'proud tyrant' associated with Kent who seems in fact to have held sway over a much larger area of the country and been virtual King of England. He managed to unify a British federation against Germanic aggressors for many years, but made the mistake his Roman predecessors had made: by inviting Saxons in and reaching a compromise which he hoped would guaranteed peace, he opened the doors to an influx which was to suffocate his own people. The newcomers staged a murderous

A detail from a fourth-century mosaic found at Rudston villa.

This primitive figure of Venus flanked by a merman comes from Rudston villa.

revolt which won them the whole of Kent and sent many more refugees on their way out of the country.

Late in the fifth century the defiant Roman-educated Britons looked for leadership to a well-born Welsh border chieftain named Ambrosius Aurelianus, who re-established contact with the shaky Western Empire, assembled a scratch fleet, and maintained what a Latin historian of the time called prosperity within Britain. Not content with holding the fort, Ambrosius chose to sally forth: attacking a Saxon army at Mount Badon (a spot with which many towns and villages today claim to be identified) he inflicted a crushing defeat.

Yet it is not the name of Ambrosius which we

associate with this or other deeds of valour. To the English, Welsh and Bretons, the legendary hero has always been King Arthur. It is highly doubtful whether any such person ever existed; but there is reason to think that ten or a dozen such persons did exist. A single monarch could hardly have spent so much time in Cornwall or Somerset while at the same time being a Welsh princeling; nor could he have been far into Scotland one day, acquitting himself in the Midlands the next, and putting new heart into the residents along Hadrian's Wall a short while after. There are tales about him at Sewingshields on the Wall, and Camboglanna (Birdoswald) has been claimed as the battlefield of Camlann. Local legend places him and Guinevere in a cave under Sewingshields Crags with his knights, ready to awaken in England's hour of greatest need. This is hard luck on Glastonbury in Somerset, which has for long made a similar claim. What is most feasible is that a number of Romanized British chieftains and client kings put up a spirited resistance in their own regions of the country over a long period before giving way under the remorseless attrition of the Anglo-Saxons, leaving behind them folk memories of chivalrous commanders blended into one symbol as King Arthur.

In the end they failed. The old system broke down. Communications were ruptured. Roads were neglected, soon became overgrown, and lost their surface metalling. Bridges collapsed. The Saxons did not like Roman methods, Roman buildings, or Roman highways. They made their own homes and their own tracks, and left the older ones to decay. The forts of the Saxon Shore became empty shells. Canals and drainage schemes silted up or reverted to swamp, aided in the Fens by a slight rise in sea level which flooded the reclaimed land. Although the Saxons preferred timber to stone, their successors did not hesitate to rob Hadrian's Wall of blocks for their farms and field walls: the Moot Hall in Hexham was created almost entirely from this source, and the pele tower in Corbridge also, though Corbridge seems to have survived for a time as an outpost of the British resistance movement under some local chief of a sub-Roman administration. In the aisle of Chollerton church are monoliths taken from Chesters, and its font was fashioned from an altar dedicated to Jupiter. In subsequent centuries a tower at Housesteads was to be the lair of border reivers or cattle thieves. The stonework of Great Chesterford in Essex was at some time carted off for road-making, while some of its pillars went into Ickleton church to support the nave arches, and some of its tiles into the church tower.

Although contacts between Christian prelates here and in Rome continued for a considerable time, there seems to have been a resurgence of paganism, not imported by the Saxons but of much older vintage – last appeals, perhaps, to old gods whose neglect may have been regarded as the cause of the current decline. Late temples appeared on Chanctonbury in Sussex and on other ancient hill-top sites. Before the Romans finally washed their hands of Britain the area of one of their iron ore workings had become a new cult centre, and it functioned long after they had gone. At Lydney, close to signal stations set up to watch for Irish raiders in the Bristol Channel, a shrine was built within an old hill-fort in honour of Nodens. This god, being also a favourite of the Irish, might have been expected either to exert himself in favour of peaceful coexistence or, equated as he was with Mars, to bestow military supremacy on his worshippers. Votive offerings of more than 8000 coins have been found there, and a mosaic was dedicated by a Roman officer from a nearby naval station. Baths and a hostel with meditation rooms were provided for pilgrims. It may also have been at this time of stress that the shrine at Maiden Castle was hastily dedicated.

All to no avail. Neither manpower nor the power of the gods could prevail against the Anglo-Saxons, surging over the land and drowning what the Romans had left behind. Even place-names which had served for 300 years were submerged beneath new ones which remain little changed to this day. Only a few cantonal capitals and other sizeable places retained faint echoes of Rome, when the newcomers adapted the Latin *castra* into *ceaster*, *caster*, or *chester* to denote a fortified town or city of Romanized character. Corinium became Cirencester, from the original Celtic name of the river Churn; Mamucium became Manchester; and Camulodunum abandoned its god Camulos and took the name of the river Colne to form Colchester. Lindum's *colonia* clung remarkably closely to its sources in becoming Lincoln.

The Latin *portus*, a port, and its related *porta*, a gate, are still with us. With the addition of *castra* we have the name of Portchester, once Portus Adurni, summing up its Roman function. The 'port' of Portus Lemanis, however, disappeared altogether

Hypocaust of the pilgrims' accommodation by the shrine of Nodens at Lydney, Gloucestershire.

The entrance to a shaft of the iron mines, also at Lydney.

and leaves us with only the corruption of Lympne. Cataractonium in the north was clearly related to the numerous waterfalls in that Pennine region, and is still recognizable as Catterick.

A number of formations retain a Celtic rather than a Latin root. Letocetum was a Celtic-Roman mixture which kept its first element when the Saxons added *feld*, meaning open land, and turned the name into Lichfield. Early British river names have survived longer than purely Roman ones. And to show that a few of the British themselves managed to survive, it is significant that the Anglo-Saxon name for a village near Piercebridge in County Durham was Walworth, thus categorizing it as an enclosure of the *walas* – 'foreigners', meaning in effect Britons or the Welsh – or more simply a homestead of Britons.

Tracing the whereabouts of the Britannic province's renamed towns is less arduous than tracing its road system, but the enthusiast can still enjoy following tracks over field and hill, and studying the reasons for modern planners' use of certain old routes and their neglect of others. Parish boundaries and hedgerows (those which have not been grubbed up to simplify modern intensive farming) often follow Roman roads. Many an upland which has escaped exploitation as arable land carries the ridge of an *agger*, even if in some cases this embankment has been reduced to little more than a smoothed-off swelling like the top of a half-buried pipeline.

Names of roads, like those of towns, have been lost or corrupted. The Saxons preferred their own trackways to the stony Roman thoroughfares and used the suffix 'streat' for anything with a paved or metalled surface, which accounts for the confusing number of Stone Streets in only slightly varying forms. Watling Street and the Icknield Way are Anglo-Saxon, though a hint of the Iceni may linger in Icknield and in the village of Ickleton in Cambridgeshire. Watling Street took its name from the Waeclingas, Wacol's people; and part of Ermine Street was in the territory of Earn's people, the Earningas. One Latin name which does seem to survive in company with its road, the Via Devana, is unfortunately a pseudo-classical concoction of the eighteenth century, attributed in the belief that the Cambridgeshire road led to a junction with the main road to Deva (Chester).

So the legions had gone for ever. Their marching roads were overgrown, their forts deserted and their townships neglected, some to revive in a later era, some to be swallowed by farmland. For us today there is perhaps more comfort in the thought of those buried ruins than in the sight of adaptations and redevelopments. It is good to know that Silchester and the great Woodchester mosaic lie sheltered under the soil; and touching to have occasional glimpses of people who tried to go on living a cultured life and to keep up their homes and communities right to the end, refusing to believe in the collapse of society or in impending war and destruction – just as we in our own time prefer not to believe in such horrors.

In the eighteenth century a patch of mosaic flooring was exposed in the Darent valley in Kent while holes were being sunk for a deer fence. Nobody followed up the discovery until 1949, when archaeological investigation uncovered the spacious villa of Lullingstone. Set on a terrace above a garden which sloped gently towards the river, it started life as a wooden farmhouse before the end of the first century and then was subjected to a number of transformations, right through to the fifth century. A rustic pagan temple was added on the terrace. Timber gave way to stone. Gradually the place took on the aspect of a desirable country residence with all modern conveniences – a bath suite, and what has been called a Deep Room, with colourful plaster panels and a sunken receptacle for spring water. A painting of water nymphs and the existence of this bowl in a lavish tiled setting suggest a cult worship of water spirits.

After a period of inexplicable neglect, when the residents moved out but someone set up a small tannery on the premises, a new family must have moved in, bringing with them some grandiose portrait busts which may have represented their ancestors, and installing their own votive pots. In the fourth century a combined temple and mausoleum was built behind the house to hold the bodies of a young couple in lead coffins accompanied by glassware, cutlery, flagons, and – to while away eternity – 30 glass gaming pieces. Rich mosaic flooring in the house itself showed Bellerophon upon Pegasus, Europa's abduction by Jupiter in the guise of a bull, and a number of swastika and leaf patterns.

The villa did not remain pagan. At some stage the occupants must have become especially fervent Christians, since they rebuilt part of the property to accommodate a set of rooms above the Deep Room,

A reconstruction of Lullingstone in its final years with its pagan temple-mausoleum on the top left.

Within this shelter are the fourth-century Lullingstone mosaics of Jupiter, and also Bellerophon.

Detail of the Bellerophon panel, with four dolphins and corner medallions of the four Seasons.

Frescoes from the chapel at Lullingstone of richly clad figures with arms outstretched in prayer.

A Chi-rho *monogram at Lullingstone chapel. There was an outer door for Christian neighbours.*

reserved for Christian worship. Walls of the main chapel were painted with praying figures and large *Chi-rho* monograms, and this symbol appeared again in the ante-chamber. The chapel is the only known example of its kind incorporated within a Romano-British villa. Just as noteworthy is the fact that while devotions were being offered here, pagan rites were still observed in the Deep Room below.

One hopes that the owners who lived in such comfort and piety – of whatever sect – and enjoyed so much of the richer pleasures of life had left before the final despoiling of their treasures. In the fifth century, fire swept through the building – the result of a Saxon raid, or careless stoking of the furnace for the hypocaust? The chapel collapsed into the pagan sanctuary, wall decorations were scorched and fragmented, and long after the charred shell had been abandoned its ruins were robbed for building materials.

Like so many kindred sites, Lullingstone is now only an echo chamber of remote, evocative resonances from a distant era.

Greek marble bust from Lullingstone, probably representing a distinguished Roman ancestor of the owner.

PLACES TO VISIT

Lullingstone, Kent
See chapter on South and South-East for location.

Saxon Shore Forts
See chapters on South and South-East, and Midlands and East Anglia for locations.
  Bradwell, Essex.
  Burgh Castle, Norfolk.

Lympne, Kent.
Pevensey, Sussex.
Portchester, Hampshire.
Reculver, Kent.
Richborough, Kent.

Scarborough, North Yorkshire
See chapter on York and the North for location.

South Cadbury Castle, Somerset, which was occupied early in the Stone Age, sacked by Vespasian, crowned by a late Celtic temple, and refortified with a massive rampart c. 500 AD. In legend it has been identified with King Arthur's Camelot.

ACKNOWLEDGMENTS

Illustrations have been reproduced by kind permission of the following:

Aerofilms Ltd: 14–15, 48, 55, 64, 68

Janet and Colin Bord: 65 top, 76 top and bottom, 81, 94, 101 top, 102, 106, 110, 115 top, 116, 117, 119, 133, 135, 149

British Museum: frontispiece, 13 left, 27, 34 top, 57, 87 top right and centre, 88 top left and bottom left, 89 top and bottom, 90, 126, 138, 139 top, 139 bottom left and right

Cambridge University Aerial Survey: 59 top, 82 top and bottom

Cambridge University Museum of Archaeology: 85 top and bottom

Carlisle Museum: 123

Central Office of Information: 18

Peter Clayton: 8 top and bottom, 50 top, 58, 60 top and bottom, 73 top, 92, 103 top, 113, 114 bottom, 127, 129 top and bottom, 144 top and bottom, 146 bottom, 147 bottom, 148 top

Colchester and Essex Museum: 30, 31, 32, 34 bottom, 84 bottom

Colchester Borough Council: 84 top

Corinium Museum, Cirencester: 51 bottom left

Department of the Environment: 100 top, 115 bottom, 118 bottom, 146 top

University of Durham: 122 bottom

Fishbourne Roman Palace: 49, 52, 53

Fotobank/England Scene: 72 top, 104 (ETB), 108

Michael Holford: copyright page, 6, 9, 16, 17 bottom, 35, 36–7, 54 top, 62, 69, 70, 71 top and bottom, 72 bottom left and right, 80, 124 top and bottom

A.F. Kersting: 20 top and bottom, 21 bottom, 50 bottom

Lady Lever Art Gallery: 26 bottom

Mansell Collection: 11, 91, 111

S & O Mathews: endpapers, 46, 51 top, 54 bottom, 75 bottom, 83, 128

Museum of Antiquities, Newcastle upon Tyne: 122 top left and top right (Phaidon Picture Archive)

Museum of London: 23 right, 26 top, 38 top, 39 bottom left and right, 40, 41, 43, 45

National Museum of Antiquities, Scotland: 23 left

National Museum of Wales: 29

National Trust: 73 bottom, 74, 101 bottom

Cressida Pemberton-Piggot: 95, 100 bottom left, 105, 107

Pictorial Colour Slides: 13, 65 bottom, 66, 67 left and right, 87 bottom, 88 top right, 93, 125, 147 top

Reading Museum: 56 bottom, 59 bottom left and right

Shrewsbury Borough Museum Service: 75 top, 77 top

Society of Antiquaries: 63 right (Phaidon Picture Archive)

Edwin Smith: 39 top, 42 bottom, 86, 100 bottom right, 103 bottom, 141, 142

Verulamium Museum: 38 bottom

Warburg Institute: 22, 33, 114 top, 136–7, 148 bottom (Phaidon Picture Archive)

Weidenfeld and Nicolson Archives: 7, 12, 42, 56 top, 63 left, 134

Derek Widdicombe: 78, 132

Andy Williams: 24, 120–1

Woodmansterne Ltd: 17 top (Colchester and Essex Museum), 19 (Museum of London), 96 top and bottom, 98 and 99 (Yorkshire Museum, photos Clive Friend FIIP)

Worth, David: 10, 44, 112, 118, 130, 131

York Archaeological Trust: 97

INDEX